TIME APART
FOR MY SOUL

Time Apart
for
My Soul

Daily Readings & Reflection for the Christian Year

Mary Zimmer

DIMENSIONS
FOR LIVING
NASHVILLE

TIME APART FOR MY SOUL
Daily Readings & Reflection for the Christian Year
Copyright © 1998 by Dimensions for Living

All rights reserved.

This book is printed on acid-free paper.

Library of Congress Cataloging-in-Publication Data

Zimmer, Mary, 1947–
    Time apart for my soul : daily readings & reflection for the Christian year / Mary Zimmer.
        p. cm.
    ISBN 0-687-05517-2 (pbk. : alk. paper)
    1. Church year meditations   I. Title.
    BV30.Z55   1998
    242'.3—dc21

98-26007
CIP

Scripture quotations, unless otherwise noted, are from the New Revised Standard Version Bible. Copyright © 1989 by the Division of Christian Education of the National Council of the Churches of Christ in the United States of America.

98 99 00 01 02 03 04 05 06 07—10 9 8 7 6 5 4 3 2 1

MANUFACTURED IN THE UNITED STATES OF AMERICA

To

the people of God known as

Crescent Hill Baptist Church

Louisville, Kentucky

Contents

Acknowledgments

The Sisters of Loretto Motherhouse and Retreat Center sits among the rolling hills of south central Kentucky. It has been my habit to go there for private retreats for a number of years. Surrounded by tall old trees, calm ponds, and open fields, I have kept retreat journals during my stays. So many of the reflections in this book refer to places and times at Loretto.

First, I would like to thank Elaine Prevalete, Retreat Director, and the Sisters of Loretto for their stewardship, which makes such a quiet, nourishing place available. To visit Loretto is to know a strong hint of what is meant by the peace of God.

I also thank the ministers and members of the people of God known as Crescent Hill Baptist Church to whom this book is dedicated. Crescent Hill has been the cradle of my adult faith for twenty-seven years in its music, Bible study, worship, preaching, and emotional and spiritual nurture. Solidarity Sunday School Class has been a church within the church for me and my family.

I thank Molly T. Marshall, pastoral teacher, sister in Christ, and dear friend for abiding encouragement and support.

I thank ministers who are friends and friends who minister to me: Bill Rogers, Bill Johnson, Ron Sisk, Bobbie Thomason, and June Hobbs.

I thank my brother-in-law, Craig Hamilton, whose gift of a computer made the writing possible.

I thank Steve Zimmer who offered steady support. I thank my sons Jacob and Michael who cheer my heart everyday.

I thank my God for all of you.

Introduction

I dwell in Possibility—
A fairer House than Prose—
More numerous of Windows—
Superior—for Doors—

Of Chambers as the Cedars—
Impregnable of Eye—
And for an Everlasting Roof
The Gambrels of the Sky—

Of Visitors—the fairest—
For Occupation—This—
The spreading wide my narrow Hands
To gather Paradise—

The author of the poem, Emily Dickinson, withdrew voluntarily what we would consider the normal relationships of family and community life. Out of that solitude and social isolation, she wrote hundreds of lyrical and evocative poems, which established her as one of America's premier poets of the nineteenth century.

Few of us would choose that level of withdrawal. The great majority of us accept the real limitations of our commitments in exchange for relationships and personal growth. But there comes a time for all of us to withdraw from the everyday schedule in order to seek God's presence in our lives. We need the solitude, which is the wide-open, spacious house of possibility in prayer.

Sincere prayer is always open to the inbreaking of the Holy Spirit and thus prayer is always a place of possibility. This place of possibility is not infinite. We are finite human beings; and thus are limited by our imaginations, our personal history, our current responsibilities, and the degree of our willingness to be open to the Holy Spirit in prayer.

But a heart open to the Spirit of God is a heart open to possibility.

INTRODUCTION

Whatever we long for, whatever we need, whatever we hope for can be brought into the realm of prayer because prayer is the spiritual gift and discipline in which we are encouraged to fervently seek the providential grace, mercy, and love of God.

Dickinson describes possibility as a dwelling place; prayer is also a dwelling place. It is the place where we dwell with God, where we know the companionship of God, and where our devoted friendship with God is nurtured. Prayer is the dwelling place that lets us question God, as well as thank and praise God. In our questions and in our seeking is possibility. Prayer always offers the possibility of growing a deeper, more vibrant faith, of wrestling with our doubts, even dreaming our dreams and learning better how to live into hope.

This book is organized by weekly chapters that are based in the seasons and themes of the Christian year. Each week has a psalm for the week, suggested daily Scripture readings, a short meditation on the weekly theme, and a guided prayer. One approach to the book would entail reading the psalm and scripture each day, reflecting on the meditation and living with it during the week, then doing the guided prayer at the end of the week. Feel free to use any approach that makes you comfortable.

One purpose of this book is to introduce the seasons and themes of the Christian year to sincere Christians who have not known about them or previously observed them. The early church based the pattern used here on the life of Jesus Christ. So, to follow the seasons of the Christian year in prayer and worship is to commemorate in each of our human lives the events of the life of Christ with the spiritual disciplines appropriate to each. For example, Advent begins four Sundays before Christmas and is focused on anticipation of the birth of Jesus. Lent begins on Ash Wednesday and continues through Holy Week, emphasizing confession and repentance.

First Sunday of Advent	Begins Year		
November 29, 1998	A	November 30, 2003	C
November 28, 1999	B	November 28, 2004	A
December 3, 2000	C	November 27, 2005	B
December 2, 2001	A	December 3, 2006	C
December 1, 2002	B		

INTRODUCTION

As in any devotional guide, this book intends to provide a focus for Scripture reading throughout the week. The meditations are reflections on one person's spiritual pilgrimage, which it is hoped will resonate with the reader's life and faith experience.

Finally, each chapter includes what is called a Guided Prayer based on the theme for the week. This is the method that emphasizes the theme of possibility in prayer. We pray hoping for God's providential intervention in our lives and in the lives of those whose names we offer in intercession. Through the use of open-ended sentences and questions in prayer, the reader is invited and encouraged to consider some of the elements of each weekly theme in an explicit and immediate form.

Please consider all of the parts of each chapter as possibilities in themselves. Prayer is one of the most important spiritual disciplines, but private prayer with meditation is one of the hardest disciplines to make a priority in our lives. Sincere prayer must be honest supplication from our own individual hearts and faith journeys. Please give yourself permission to use the sections of each chapter as they feel comfortable to you.

May you find in your prayers a renewed sense of possibility in the depths of your faith and across the breadth of your life.

TIME APART
FOR MY SOUL

ADVENT

HOPE

Psalm 42

Daily Scripture

* Sunday:

A	B	C
Isaiah 2:1-5	Isaiah 64:1-9	Jeremiah 33:14-16
Psalm 122	Psalm 80:1-7, 17-19	Psalm 25:1-10
Romans 13:11-14	1 Corinthians 1:3-9	1 Thessalonians 3:9-13
Matthew 24:36-44	Mark 13:24-37	Luke 21:25-36

*Monday:	Jeremiah 29:10-14
* Tuesday:	Psalm 130
* Wednesday:	Proverbs 23:15-18
* Thursday:	Matthew 12:15-21
* Friday:	Romans 5:1-5
* Saturday:	Romans 8:18-27

Meditation

The first Wednesday of Advent in 1993, my son called from school to tell me that three boys from his school had been expelled for possession of handguns. One had offered to let Michael hold his gun. Michael refused, but what alarmed me was that Michael was not scared since "the gun was unloaded, Mom."

The incident happened just after Hope Sunday in Advent. There had been a story each day in the paper that week about guns being used to kill family members and strangers because someone was enraged and had access to a weapon. Two were preschoolers killed by their father.

I wondered how we could teach hope in a world where guns come to school in backpacks. The beginning of an answer came on a drizzling morning two days later as I was on my way to chapel.

On a stretch of dogwood branches there were plump raindrops clinging to the bare twigs. I thought about rain and moisture and how fear makes both our mouths and hearts go dry. What we need are the drops of moist hope in these fear-filled days in a scary world.

It seems an incredulous comparison—an impossible standoff: drops of rain against the dark metal of guns and bullets. But that's what all hope is. It is ephemeral because hope comes from the unknown of God in our lives. Hope comes from beyond us, from the not-yet-imagined possibilities in our lives.

We all need hope. Hope to live by. Hope to get by. Hope that tomorrow will be better. Hope that one day we will hope again. Hope is as fragile as raindrops against guns, as fragile as God's moisture in the face of human rage.

Thus all we can do for hope is to be open to it. We cannot create it for ourselves or others though we may all serve as channels of hope for one another. For the coming of hope into our hearts and lives in any dark day, we must be able to open our hearts and lives to the unknown of God, to not-yet-imagined providence, to the fragility of raindrops on dogwood twigs, and to a daily prayer of possibility.

Guided Prayer

Dear God,

My barriers to hope this Advent are ——————————

———————————————————————————

———————————————————————————

———————————————————————————

———————————————————————————.

I need to hope again because ——————————————

———————————————————————————

———————————————————————————

———————————————————————————

———————————————————————————.

The place in my life where hope is most important is———————

———————————————————————————

———————————————————————————

———————————————————————————

———————————————————————————.

Please bring the moisture of hope into my dry faith. Come, holy Jesus. You are needed in my life and faith. Grant me the humility of shepherds as I seek your shining face. Amen.

JOY

Psalm 16

Daily Scripture

* Sunday:

A	B	C
Isaiah 11:1-10	Isaiah 40:1-11	Baruch 5:1-9
Psalm 72:1-7, 18-19	Psalm 85:1-2, 8-13	or Malachi 3:1-4
Romans 15:4-13	2 Peter 3:8-15, 18	Luke 1:68-79
Matthew 3:1-12	Mark 1:1-8	Philippians 1:3-11
		Luke 3:1-6

* Monday:	Psalm 51:6-12
* Tuesday:	Psalm 65
* Wednesday:	Isaiah 35:1-10
* Thursday:	Isaiah 55:6-13
* Friday:	Luke 1:39-55
* Saturday:	John 16:20-24

Meditation

"Oh Joy that seekest me through pain.
I cannot close my heart to thee . . ."
George Matheson

This Advent, joy is cerise-pink clouds in the sky. On the Friday before Joy Sunday, I go to walk at the reservoir. Dark comes early and a wind is blowing before the clouds roll in. But beneath dark gray, rolling clouds, the sun refuses to be darkened. There is a streak of ruby light on the horizon fading to yellow-orange at the far edges. And briefly, oh-so-briefly, the ruby color pans out beneath the charcoal clouds and turns their underneath side a glowing, vibrant rose-pink.

The color fades, of course. The bright colors of sunset and paler washes of dusk always fade before the night.

I have long considered joy's presence in our lives as much like the happenstance of grace. Joy breaks in, drops in and flies. We cannot create it, no matter how many magic plastic credit cards we have. We cannot capture and hold joy for warmth and light in darker times.

In those times, we can remember joy. We can remember the squeals of delight we hear from children on Christmas morning or their voices raised in carols for the Christmas program. We can remember the light in a loved one's eyes, grateful for one more shared Christmas. We can cherish the sight of a sanctuary filled with candles on Christmas Eve while "Silent Night" fills the air.

But we cannot recreate those times on cue. The hymn writer gives us a clue—that we never close our hearts to joy. There are many things that close our hearts to joy—old, nursed grievances, the fantasy of revenge, unmediated anger, unconfessed sin, unreflected fear. We may know we have closed our hearts, or we may only be aware that life holds little anticipation and virtually no giggles.

But there is always the possibility of change—of the choice to be open, of a renewed sense of life. There is always the possibility of joy; all that is required is a heart open to the presence of joy in the world.

Getting open may be a process. In order to have an open heart, we start with reflection and confession. We search the prisons, the closed-off places, the murky, crowded closets of our hearts.

Guided Prayer

Dear God,

This season of joy, I need to open my heart to joy because _____

_____

_____

_____

_____

_____

_____.

Though joy is fleeting, I look for joy since _____

_____

_____

_____

_____

_____

_____.

What is the barrier to joy within me this Advent? Search my heart, O God, and take away anger, resentment, or jealousy which take up room where your joy seeks to lodge.

When joy crosses my path, stop me in my tracks, O God. Let me savor the blessing of joy, which is a gift of your grace. Amen.

PEACE

Psalm 23

Daily Scripture

* Sunday:

A	B	C
Isaiah 35:1-10	Isaiah 61:1-4, 8-11	Zephaniah 3:14-20
Psalm 146:5-10	Psalm 126 or Luke 1:47-55	Isaiah 12:2-6
or Luke 1:47-55	1 Thessalonians 5:16-24	Philippians 4:4-7
James 5:7-10	John 1:6-8, 19-28	Luke 3:7-18
Matthew 11:2-11		

* Monday:	Luke 1:68-79
* Tuesday:	Psalm 34
* Wednesday:	Zechariah 8:11-19
* Thursday:	Isaiah 9:2-7
* Friday:	Isaiah 55:6-13
* Saturday:	John 14:15-27

Meditation

Crescent Hill Baptist Church hosts a bereavement worship service on the third Sunday of Advent every year. The tradition began the year that one of the most vibrant, outgoing young women in our youth group was killed in a car accident on her way to school one foggy October morning. Out of our corporate shock and grief, a specific time was set aside. The bereavement service is a chance for those who have a significant loss to come together in a quiet service of mourning and, it is hoped, a renewed sense of peace.

Personal and social peace is a rare treasure in our contemporary world. Peace is perhaps the most elusive quality of Advent as we scurry to buy, wrap, mail, bake, party, decorate, and celebrate the season.

In times of loss or pain or emotional agitation, the Twenty-third Psalm is probably the first and most common source of scriptural consolation. It is so familiar that it is easy to dismiss the weight of its meaning. Because we are impatient and hurried in American society, it's often difficult for us to slow down and pay attention. "Waiting on the Lord" is a common scriptural injunction, but it is perhaps the hardest for the American psyche.

A brief look at Psalm 23 shadows the dependence of the speaker on God. God is the primary actor; the person receives what God gives. There are eight verbs that describe what God does: shepherds, makes me lie, leads me, restores me, is present with me, comforts, prepares a table, and anoints. The human speaker walks, fears no evil, and dwells. Perhaps it is this proportion that scares us in our responsible, activist roles and individualist cultural mores. For God has the great preponderance of action in this psalm devoted to the assurance of care and peace.

Could it be that our cries for "peace, peace, when there is no peace" are related to our need to be in control and in charge? What if peace is that elusive spiritual gift which only has a chance to be given by God when we relinquish control and are in a simple, receptive mode? It is frightening to actually, truly "let go and let God." But if the hands of our spiritual life are clenched in control or dread, we cannot open them to receive peace.

Guided Prayer

Dear God,

Today, I am anxious about _____

_____

_____

_____.

I need the gift of your peace because_____

_____

_____

_____.

I confess that I still want to control_____

_____

_____

_____.

Will you show me the way out of this urge to be in control over what is truly a need to wait on the movement of your Spirit?

Peace is so elusive in our world. Today I pray for peace in _____

_____. And I pray for peace between_____ who are estranged.

Grant us all, O Lord, the peace of a quiet, stable calm in the morning light. Amen.

LOVE

Psalm 116

Daily Scripture

* Sunday:

A	B	C
Isaiah 7:10-16	2 Samuel 7:1-11, 16	Micah 5:2-5*a*
Psalm 80:1-7, 17-19	Luke 1:47-55 or	Luke 1:47-55
Romans 1:1-7	Psalm 89:1-4, 19-26	or Psalm 80:1-7
Matthew 1:18-25	Romans 16:25-27	Hebrews 10:5-10
	Luke 1:26-38	Luke 1:39-45

* Monday:	1 Corinthians 13:1-13
* Tuesday:	Romans 8:28-37
* Wednesday:	John 15:1-17
* Thursday:	John 21:15-17
* Friday:	Matthew 22:34-40
* Saturday:	Luke 6:27-36

Meditation

Remember the JOY formula? Most of us learned it when we were young, and the positive intent was that we would be less selfish. We were to remember the order of the letters in the acronym: Jesus, Others, You. And we were to make that order our priority in relationships and behavior.

I began to wonder if this was not some kind of spiritual bargain that we tried to make with God. That is, if we really and truly ever do figure out how to put Jesus and others absolutely before ourselves, then will it be all right to love ourselves?

A primary tenet of pastoral care is that we recognize the presumption in the Golden Rule: loving one another as we love ourselves implies that we learn healthy self-respect and self-regard first. And most of us *do* love others as we love ourselves. Often it is not nearly enough.

One of the wisdoms of maturity is recognizing that loving others is truly more crucial than having proof that others love us. The heart that does not love is a dying heart. The impulse to reach out to others in compassion is what keeps our hearts soft and warm, what makes us feel actually alive.

One of the lessons of the Creation story in Genesis is that we are made to love. God wanted companionship, connection, and relation; and we are made in the image of a God who seeks connection and relationship.

Sadly, American consumer culture has diminished the meaning of our one English word *love* until many commonly equate this word only with sexual attraction. We need to reclaim the word as one that conveys our reaching out to others in the basic human connection of understanding friendship first of all, then the affirming of familial devotion we have to a few people, and finally the welling up of compassion for the suffering ones we meet.

These are the dimensions of agape love, the love that Jesus modeled to friends and even ostensible foes. But there is a preliminary step for the rest of us mortals. That step is coming to the acceptance of God's unequivocal and limitless love for us. Such love is a reservoir of streams of mercy and springs of grace always welling up for our thirsty, depleted souls.

The monastic tradition has taught us that we must return to that reservoir again and again, in solitude, silence, and simplicity. Thereby we will be filled and nourished, enabled once again to go out in love for others.

Guided Prayer

Dear God,

There always seems to be too little love to go around. What has stopped up love in me? I would love _____

_____

_____

_____ more humbly. I would

love _____

_____

_____

_____ more thoroughly.

Soften my heart in these days of carols and bells. Make the deepest parts of my soul open to receive the love you and others have to offer me. Let such love grow until I am full to overflowing and then show me where to pour out the love that has grown within. Amen.

EPIPHANY

BEGINNINGS

Psalm 111

Daily Scripture

* Sunday:

A	B	C
Isaiah 63:7-9	Isaiah 61:10–62:3	1 Samuel 2:18-20, 26
Psalm 148	Psalm 148	Psalm 148
Hebrews 2:10-18	Galatians 4:4-7	Colossians 3:12-17
Matthew 2:13-23	Luke 2:22-40	Luke 2: 41-52

* Monday:	Genesis 1
* Tuesday:	Proverbs 8:22-36
* Wednesday:	Isaiah 48:12-17
* Thursday:	Luke 4:14-24
* Friday:	John 1:1-5
* Saturday:	Acts 9:1-19

Meditation

I grew up in a family whose life revolved around the school calendar rather than the annual one. So I have often felt that a new year, symbolized by new school supplies and new classes, truly began on the cusp of August and September. I used to spend New Year's Eve in the standard way—at a party with friends, complete with carefully saved hats and handfuls of new streamers to throw at one another until we were all decorated.

The tradition of New Year's resolutions makes good sense. But too often the tradition is a fairly empty one and the resolutions do not result in a serious turning in our lives. The connotation of resolutions is often one of quitting bad habits, rather than making a fresh start.

The pace of our lives is such that the week between Christmas and New Year's, which can be a quiet time for reflection, is often a time of simply reestablishing routines; and those routines themselves are often connected to the fresh start we need. But the routines may also be the biggest barrier to a new beginning.

Perhaps it is the pressure we put on ourselves about New Year's resolutions. Perhaps it is the easy rationales that come when we don't follow through, or we break down quickly in our resolve and then just give up. Because it is human to resist change, even the change we need, we often have good intentions that don't result in significant new beginnings.

The etymology of the root of the word *resolution* is important: *resolve* comes from a word that means to loosen. The first dictionary definition of *resolution* is "reducing to a simpler form." Perhaps that is the clue to New Year's resolutions. The question is not, "What do I change about myself so I will be a better, more likable, or thinner person?"

The questions for new beginnings are, "What in my life needs to be reduced to a more simple form? In what area of life do I need to get back to basics? What has bound me up, and what do I need to loosen? What responsibility or load or compulsion do I simply need to let go?"

New beginnings are a matter of change. And real change is not instantaneous. Perhaps we need to ponder not only the loosening and simplifying we need to do, but also what the new beginning will change in our lives and how we will incorporate—how we will *embody* that change.

Guided Prayer

Dear God,

I am bound up in my life right now by _____

_____

_____

_____.

I need to let go of _____

_____

_____

_____.

Please loosen the quality of _____ in
me.

In the time of new beginnings, I want to know the beginning of
new vibrancy in my faith. Grant me patience as I seek those ways in
which you will lead me to a year of deepened faith. Amen.

ANTICIPATION

Psalm 43

Daily Scripture

* Sunday:

A	B	C
Isaiah 60:1-6	Isaiah 60:1-6	Isaiah 60:1-6
Psalm 72:1-7,10-14	Psalm 72:1-7,10-14	Psalm 72:1-7, 10-14
Ephesians 3:1-12	Ephesians 3:1-12	Ephesians 3:1-12
Matthew 2:1-12	Matthew 2:1-12	Matthew 2:1-12

* Monday: Isaiah 2:2-5 and 9:2
* Tuesday: Matthew 2;1-12
* Wednesday: Isaiah 58:8-11
* Thursday: Luke 8:16-17
* Friday: John 1:1-5
* Saturday: Hebrews 12:1-2

Meditation

The season of Epiphany celebrates the birth of Jesus as the coming of God's redemptive Light into a world dark with human intrigue, hate, and abusive power. The story of the wise men who had "seen a star" and lived in anticipation of seeing the new king of the Jews is the traditional story of Epiphany. One of the most significant aspects of this time in the Christian year is that the season of Christmas is extended into the new secular year, and we are invited to ask ourselves a question about the birth of the Christ Child in our world. The question is, Now what?

What do we do now with this good news? Renewed by the joy of Christmas once again, what do we anticipate in our lives as disciples of Christ and in our communal life together as the church?

Have you ever taken a night hike? With just the gleam of a flashlight in front of you, the fervent hope is that this particular battery-powered light will shine into the darkness and not be overcome until you are safely back to a campfire. Nocturnal animals make furtive noises and branches crack. You really don't know what is out there in front of, beside, or behind you.

Some of us feel this way about the future. We begin each new year without much sense of anticipation because we have learned to fear rather than anticipate the unknown of the future. To anticipate is to expect, to be expectant. Anticipation is one aspect of hope; if we cannot even anticipate something in our future, we are not likely to feel hope.

Perhaps part of the problem is believing that we are totally on our own, responsible for the light that accompanies us in the darkness. We may not take the first step until we are certain that we have just the right flashlight with brand-new batteries. Consequently, the adventure of a night hike and the revelations that the future has to offer us are postponed.

The message of Epiphany is that God has created light in our world and has Light to offer to our hearts. Just as the sun, moon, and stars shine in the natural world, there are sources of light for our personal journey of faith into any future, no matter how dark it appears in midwinter. We do have to gather the resources, such as prayer and Scripture and community. And we do have to start out on that night hike.

Guided Prayer

Dear God,

I am afraid of the future because _____

_____

_____.

I want to be able to anticipate that _____

_____

_____.

Please bring the light of your _____

and grant me the sustenance of your grace as I face changes in this year.

Thank you for the light of each new day. Thank you for the light in the eyes that give love and friendship. On these short days of winter, show me the way to the light of your love, which lifts my heart in praise. Amen.

BAPTISM

Psalm 65

Daily Scripture

* Sunday:

A	B	C
Isaiah 42:1-9	Genesis 1:1-5	Isaiah 43:1-7
Psalm 29	Psalm 29	Psalm 29
Acts 10:34-43	Acts 9:1-7	Acts 8:14-17
Matthew 3:13-17	Mark 1:4-11	Luke 3:15-17, 21-22

* **Monday:**	Matthew 3:1-10
* **Tuesday:**	Luke 3:15-17
* **Wednesday:**	Matthew 3:13-17
* **Thursday:**	Romans 6:1-11
* **Friday:**	Jeremiah 17:5-8
* **Saturday:**	Jeremiah 31:7-12

Meditation

For Christians the symbol of baptism is a central motif for faith. The Hebrew Scriptures are full of the image of water as a symbol of God's blessings or withholding of blessing. Abundant rain and rivers flowing with water meant that crops would flourish and life for the people was secure. Drought and desert, the absence of enough water, threatened their very survival.

And John the Baptist came preaching repentance with baptism as the sign of a change of heart that turned the person once more to God. The baptism of Jesus becomes a sign of God's active presence in the world as the Holy Spirit blesses the life Jesus will live out and sacrifice.

For us today, baptism is often a sign of renewal. As Christian communities we celebrate the baptism of new persons into the church, accepting them as brothers and sisters in Christ. Welcoming each new member signifies that the church itself may be renewed by the presence of the gifts they bring.

Like other significant life events, the meaningfulness of our baptism is very individualized. If we are in the tradition of christening, we don't remember anything about it. But the obsolete meaning of the word is "Christianize, to make a Christian." And, whether in an ornate cathedral with family gathered around a font or in a stream with a choir on the bank offering call and response, baptism is about "getting washed up" as the character of Jesus describes it in the musical *Godspell*. And it always happens in community.

Though the literal event of baptism happens only once for each believer, spiritually the symbol of baptism can be one in which our spirit is renewed as often as needed on the journey. Since becoming a Christian doesn't erase our capacity to sin, most of us need to get our minds and hearts and spirits "washed up" on a regular basis.

Think about how good water feels on our skin. To wash or shower when we feel the need of cleansing our body is nearly always a good feeling. Imagine that sensation for the washing up that needs to be done for what burdens and grieves our hearts because of our behaviors that have fallen short. Imagine being thoroughly washed with forgiveness and then blessed to be sent out, renewed once more.

Guided Prayer

O God,

I come to you needing baptism for my spirit again. I have regret about_____

_____

_____.

_____

I feel burdened by my shortcoming that _____

_____

_____.

_____

I repent of my habit of _____.

Create in me a clean heart. Wash my soul once more with your constant and everlasting forgiveness. Renew a right spirit within me for Jesus' sake. Amen.

LOOKING TO THE FUTURE

Psalm 130

Daily Scripture

* Sunday:

A	B	C
Isaiah 49:1-7	1 Samuel 3:1-10	Isaiah 62:1-5
Psalm 40:1-11	Psalm 139:1-6, 13-18	Psalm 36:5-10
1 Corinthians 1:1-9	1 Corinthians 6:12-20	1 Corinthians 12:1-11
John 1:29-42	John 1:43-51	John 2:1-11

* Monday: Job 17:3-16
* Tuesday: Proverbs 13:9-13
* Wednesday: Jeremiah 29:3-14
* Thursday: Jeremiah 31:11-17
* Friday: Romans 5:1-5
* Saturday: Romans 8:19-25

Meditation

When my sister called with the news of her pregnancy, both hope and a thread of trepidation ran through me. At forty, she had waited a long time for this baby. And as a highly intelligent, dedicated career woman, she had the biggest adjustment of her life in front of her.

A few months later, I called her to tell her I had realized that I already loved my new nephew, even before he had actually arrived. He had become a symbol of hope for me because the old clichÇ is right: babies are a sign of God's intention that life should go on.

I told my bemused sons that they would have to tolerate my being really silly about this baby. I intended to be an irrationally doting aunt; extravagance in phone bills, presents, and conversation was appropriate.

After Johnathan Daniel arrived, I flew out for a weekend ostensibly to care for my sister. But I ended up doing a lot of rocking and singing to a beautiful little boy. As I rocked, I pondered his parents' anticipation of the challenges, pain, and joys of this baby's future.

The winter had been long, cold, and snowy; but here was this baby needing simple things like food, sleep, and dry pants. And I thought about how a spiritual winter makes it easy to give up on anticipation of the future, to let dread take up residence. A winter of the heart makes it easy to relinquish hope.

The good news on a cold, snowy Saturday morning is that it is never too late to learn to hope again. It is never too late to look forward to whatever future might be out there for each one of us. For people of faith, the search for faith is a necessary prerequisite to hope. In any spiritual winter we may rail at God for the dread of the future which visits us. But part of learning to hope again is praying that dread, speaking to God about what robs us of anticipation of the future.

And the faith that grows hope needs simple things too. Faith needs the food of Scripture, the rest of prayer, and friends who dry our tears with their dedication and encouragement. Faith that grows hope needs to be rocked in the rhythms of community and of hymns that rise in our hearts.

Guided Prayer

Dear God,
   Sometimes I am afraid to hope because _____
_____
_____
_____.

   What I dread most right now is _____
_____.
_____
_____

   I need the hope of renewed faith because _____
_____
_____.

   I have been searching_____
_____
_____

   I want to anticipate that _____
_____
_____

   Lead me in the path of hope, O God. Renew my faith in your providence for the future of my own life. Strengthen my faith in the depths of winter. Amen.

FAITH

Psalm 146

Daily Scripture

*** Sunday:**

A	B	C
Amos 3:1-8	Jeremiah 3:21–4:2	Nehemiah 8:2-10
Psalm 139:1-11	Psalm 130	Psalm 113
1 Corinthians 1:10-17	1 Corinthians 7:17-23	1 Corinthians 12:12-27
Matthew 4:12-23	Mark 1:14-20	Luke 4:14-21

*** Monday:**	Hebrews 11:1
*** Tuesday:**	Matthew 8:5-13
*** Wednesday:**	Romans 1:16-17
*** Thursday:**	Galatians 2:23-28
*** Friday:**	James 2:18-26
*** Saturday:**	John 11:17-27

Meditation

For a growing faith, the old adage of "seeing is believing" has to be turned on its head. Contrary to all the rhetoric about faith being mostly a matter of logical conclusion, in fact, faith is a matter of believing our way into seeing. When faith and science clashed in the nineteenth century, many people concluded that the way to faith was first the acceptance of a few basic propositions. Then the use of deductive reasoning from those propositions intended to answer all the questions that arise about the Bible and about the existence of evil in the world. Though an unintentional result, faith got divided into "heart religion" versus "head religion." And supporters of each became fairly hostile to one another.

But a vibrant, living, nurturing faith needs all the best of our whole selves. It is not a matter of heart or mind or soul, but of all those parts of our selves. To quote the theologians, we can learn to love God with our minds; and we must do so for faith to grow as our intellect and life experience grow. But the mystics teach us that we cannot stop there. We go beyond reading and reasoning and evaluation, to prayer, to reading with devotion, to seeking God's presence and grace in all of life.

The ways in which believing is seeing include knowing that there are still stars brilliant in the sky beyond a murky summer night, depending on the sun to still be there despite gray day after gray day, remembering the sap biding its time in the ghostly branches of the sycamore tree, trusting in love one more time after betrayal. The issue is how far can we see. And that is determined by how far and how hard we are looking for faith. For faith to grow, we cannot depend on what is apparent; we have to look beyond what we can see, beyond what is starkly real in our day to day lives.

Some people talk about faith as if it is easy. But it is not. Faith is hard. Nurturing and growing a faith in God's goodness and grace is a matter of a determined search conducted by a heart open to all the possibilities of that goodness and grace.

Putting our faith in other seemingly deeply spiritual persons can be a mistake. They can model faith in practice and discipline for us, but faith cannot be borrowed or exchanged.

Once I accompanied my mother on an airplane trip. She needed a wheelchair to get around the airport but could manage the airplane aisles with some help. The best way for us to travel those aisles was for me to walk backwards supporting her outstretched arms with mine. Those short, tentative jaunts gave me a metaphor for God's presence when our faith is wobbly and unsure. One crucial aspect of faith is seeing with our hearts that God goes before us, beckons us on in the journey of faith, and looks upon us with endless mercy and love.

Guided Prayer

O God,

Today my faith is like a _____

_____

_____.

I feel unsteady because _____

_____

_____.

Faith is hard to experience in my life right now since _____

_____

_____.

I need your merciful guidance so that _____

_____

_____.

Show me what is possible.

I am afraid of facing my doubts since _____

_____

_____

Growing in faith might mean that I would _____

_____

_____.

Hold out your arms of sure strength to me. I will lean and follow. Amen.

CHANGE

Psalm 46

Daily Scripture

* Sunday:

A	B	C
Micah 6:1-8	Deuteronomy 18:15-20	Jeremiah 1:4-10
Psalm 15	Psalm 111	Psalm 71:1-16
1 Corinthians 18	1 Corinthians 8:1-13	1 Corinthians 13:1-13
Matthew 5:1-12	Mark 1:21-28	Luke 4:21-30

* Monday: Job 38:4-18
* Tuesday: Isaiah 40:6-11
* Wednesday: Ezekiel 18:30-32
* Thursday: Luke 5:33-38
* Friday: Romans 7:4-6
* Saturday: 2 Corinthians 5:16-21

Meditation

You have to realize, Mary, in the South *change* is a four-letter word," my wise friend said to me when we were discussing a church crisis. I had grown up in Oklahoma where late statehood and the pioneer mentality, plus a constant wind, seemed to create an ethos that what was new and different was not to be feared. But in the Southern culture where I have spent my adulthood, I often find myself at odds with what seem the eternal ramifications of the phrase, "We've never done it that way before" as the definitive and conclusive remark about any proposed change.

When I tried to make sense of this, I realized that what I experienced as inertia was really the comfort of familiarity. The human organism and most of its organizations are resistant to change. We seek stasis. Change takes energy and effort. And the first barrier to even seriously needed change is that it is unfamiliar and uncomfortable, so our impulse for stasis immediately sets up resistance.

The irony is that even as we resist change, we are constantly in a state of change. Biologically, our bodies are constantly renewing and changing, sometimes growing, sometimes aging. And each day of our lives is different. We never step into exactly the same time or place or relationship from day to day. So change is what we live in; it is how we live.

We live in a world in which the rate of change is increasing exponentially every year. That is, there is more social, political, and economic change happening faster than ever before in human history. Thus, perhaps our resistance to change in our families, neighborhoods, and churches is a reaction to the constant, rapid change we experience in the larger world.

Spiritually the question becomes, "What needed change are we resisting?" The comfort of familiarity can lead us to idolize what we already know and practice. We can make an idol of what is and has been, and close the door to possibility in prayer and worship. Seeking God only through what is familiar allows the temptation to try to control what happens in prayer. We can also be tempted to control our relationship with God in order to prevent the inbreaking of the Spirit into our lives. The Spirit of God blows where it will, and that theological truth itself means that we cannot control what God is doing in the world or in our lives.

We can be imprisoned by the familiar. Familiarity is comfortable—or at least it provides us with the illusion of comfort. The familiar can also be an icon—a means or channel of grace, blessing, and communion. But if we never open our hearts and souls to the winds of the Spirit—if we never risk change—then faith stagnates. To be truly open to the possibility of God's working in our lives, we must risk encounter with the unfamiliar. We have to take a chance on being uncomfortable. We have to be willing to change.

Guided Prayer

Dear God,

The change I am most afraid of right now is _____

_____

_____.

The threat of that change is overwhelming because _____

_____

_____.

What change do I need to seek in my life of faith as a Christian?

_____

_____.

What winds of change does the Spirit need to blow into my prayer

life right now?_____

_____

_____.

What will be different if I open myself to change?_____

_____

_____.

What gifts and blessings of change are possible?_____

_____

_____.

Come, be near me as I anticipate change that I would not choose. Come bring me the change that enlarges my heart and my witness of your grace. Amen.

WEEK 11

TRANSFIGURATION SUNDAY

Psalm 77

Daily Scripture

*Sunday:

A	B	C
Exodus 24:12-18	2 Kings 2:1-12	Exodus 34:29-35
Psalm 99	Psalm 50:1-6	Psalm 99
2 Peter 1:16-21	2 Corinthians 4:3-6	2 Corinthians 3:12–4:2
Matthew 17:1-9	Mark 9:2-9	Luke 9:28-36

*Monday:	Mark 9:2-9
*Tuesday:	Matthew 17:1-9
*Wednesday:	Luke 9:28-36
*Thursday:	Mark 12:28-34
*Friday:	Luke 9:23-27
*Saturday:	Romans 12:1-2

Meditation

The scripture passages describing Jesus' transfiguration challenge our dependence on empirical definitions of reality. What are we supposed to make of this story? Do we have a chance of understanding what was happening any more than the early disciples did?

As in most of the dramatic events of Jesus' life, the response of the disciples is confusion and fear. Peter acknowledges Jesus' significance when he is joined by Moses and Elijah. Jesus is both prophet and savior to his people. And Peter, always the man of action, proposes a commemorative event of building three tents for the three leaders. But then these three disciples are witness to a theophany, or appearance of God in their lives. And the clear message is that Jesus is anointed Son and Messiah. The instruction from God is simple and clear: Listen to him.

Jesus was recognized as teacher and preacher, but only a few people in his lifetime actually listened to him. Their witness about experiences such as the transfiguration was so powerful that the Christian religion was the result.

The teachings of Jesus are radical and transformational. To listen to Jesus is to hear lessons that turn our usual assumptions about life and how we are to live it upside down. The changes in our lives that may happen because we listen to Jesus might be as powerful and overwhelming as witnessing a transfiguration ourselves.

Listening to Jesus on the shores of Galilee and roads leading to Jerusalem must have been a powerful experience. Disciples left their homes and families to follow him. Their whole lives were changed.

For us to listen to Jesus is to be open to the radical redemption of our lives. We are redeemed away from the world's values and led to a lifestyle and behaviors that would, if they were adopted by most people, lead to a world so different from the one we know that we would hardly recognize it. It would be as strange as a man dressed in shining white garments rising just off the edge of the earth and joined by the spirits of two prophets long gone.

To listen to Jesus is to hear the stories of the transfiguration of people's lives, of the social order and the whole purpose of human life. To listen to Jesus is to find our whole lives transformed.

Guided Prayer

O God,

Such events as the transfiguration are almost impossible for me to conceive, much less believe. Your words, "Listen to Jesus" are easy to hear and hard to follow.

I confess that I fear and resist the radical redemption offered by the gospel of Jesus Christ. The parts of my life that are not open to

transformation are _____

_____

_____.

I need to listen to Jesus about _____

_____

_____.

I need to learn better his lessons about _____

_____

_____.

The redemption I need in my life is redemption of _____

_____

_____.

May the presence of Christ as loving Teacher be with me throughout this day and week as I open my heart and life to redemption and transformation. Amen.

ZENT

CONFESSION

Psalm 51

Daily Scripture

* Sunday:

A	B	C
Genesis 2:15-17, 3:1-7	Genesis 9:8-17	Deuteronomy 26:1-11
Psalm 32	Psalm 25:1-10	Psalm 91:1-2, 9-16
Romans 5:12-19	1 Peter 3:18-22	Romans 10:8b-13
Matthew 4:1-11	Mark 1:9-15	Luke 4:1-13

* Monday: Hebrews 3:7-15
* Tuesday: Luke 15:11-24
* Wednesday: Philippians 2:5-13
* Thursday: James 5:13-16
* Friday: Romans 10:9-13
* Saturday: 1 John 4:7-21

Meditation

On retreat, during one Lenten season, I found myself confronted with my rebellion against God. Since I had grown up in a religious environment focused on following strict rules of fundamentalism, I had long worked hard to be obedient and to be "good." In fact, such an approach to faith and spiritual life had become a form of spiritual tyranny. The "tyranny of being good" as it was defined in my religious subculture had often closed down my prayer life as I tried hard to "be good" in prayer and find the "obedient" attitude and "right" words with which to pray and to experience myself heard by God.

But one day on this retreat, awareness of my own particular and current brand of rebelling against God was so acute that my throat stopped and I could hardly swallow food. What I needed to repent of this particular Lent was not my rebellion against the laws of God but my rebellion against the love of God.

The entire time that the prodigal son spent in the far country was not primarily a rebellion against the public customs or rules of his father. He was rebelling against the relationship of love, which did contain expectations he did not want to have to face.

To be loved by God and to accept the gift of that love is to become responsible for how our life is lived out as a chosen child of God. There is a lot more spiritual empowerment in that posture for a Christian than in the posture of just trying to be good and follow all the rules. Just as the love of Jesus Christ superseded the Torah, we may find that some of our lifetime assumptions about how we live as Christians are brought up for reexamination once we accept the love of God for our whole selves.

The prodigal's life after he returned would be totally different from the life he lived before he left home or the rebellious life he lived in the far country. After experiencing his father's welcoming love, he would have to respond as an adult rather than as a child.

So after a time of death in my writing life, I realized that my spiritual posture to God about the gift of words had been a flippant, "Thanks, but no thanks." To accept that gift as a part of my whole created self was to become responsible for how that gift is borne responsibly and lived out in my Christian journey. To fully accept that gift was also to accept that I was beloved of God and that nothing could separate me from the love of God.

But first, confession was necessary. Those persons who recover the gift of honest confession experience a freeing of the spirit from the tyranny of sin, even when the sin is one unimaginable earlier in an inherited scheme of "goodness." In prayer I had to acknowledge to God that I sinned by trying to deny a creative urge which was a gift, because I did not want the responsibility of that gift. Attempted denial of the gift was also a denial of the love of the Giver.

Guided Prayer

O God,

Sometimes I do not know what my confession needs to be. When I examine my life this day, the area that needs confession is _____

_____

_____

_____.

I want to be cleansed of the sin of _____

_____

_____

_____.

I need a purified heart since _____

_____

_____

_____.

Keep me constant in the awareness that I can, at anytime, anywhere, offer up my broken spirit to you. Grant me a new and steadfast spirit so that _____

_____

_____

_____.

I need and ask for your merciful forgiveness. Let me know a renewed joy of my salvation. Then I will experience gladness of heart. I will praise the justice of your righteousness and your name before all the earth. Amen.

REPENTANCE

Psalm 90

Daily Scripture

* Sunday:

A	B	C
Genesis 12:1-4*a*	Genesis 17:1-7,15-16	Genesis 15:1-12, 17-18
Psalm 121	Psalm 22:23-31	Psalm 27
Romans 4:1-5, 13-17	Romans 4:13-25	Philippians 3:17–4:1
John 3:1-17	Mark 8:31-38	Luke 13:31-35

* Monday:	Joel 2:12-13
* Tuesday:	2 Chronicles 6:36-40
* Wednesday:	Matthew 3:1-12
* Thursday:	Luke 15:3-10
* Friday:	2 Timothy 2:22-26
* Saturday:	Revelation 3:19-22

Meditation

The word *repent* conjures images of fiery evangelists hollering from the pulpit. And in the tradition of my childhood, that preaching was directed at the "unsaved"; the emphasis on the benefits of repentance was freedom from the threat of everlasting punishment in hell.

So, like many of my peers reared in such a faithful environment, I became a "good person." I signed on the list of *ought to*s and on the list of *don't ever*s (well, at least most of them) and tried to live up to the lists in my thoughts and behaviors.

Years later I discovered the spiritual discipline of confession and the freedom from the "tyranny of goodness." For repentance is not a one-time event for Christians. Repentance is one of those lessons we learn over and over. This does not mean that we ignore moral habits, but that we are able to live out of them because we want to be persons of vibrant integrity. We do not want just to avoid breaking a rule and avoid punishment.

To repent is to feel sorry for something we have done or said. And the season of Lent is a time of repentance. It is a time of "examen," as St. Ignatius would describe the needed reflection on the honesty of our thoughts, the purity of our motives, and the compassion of our behavior.

The revelation to someone reared in what functioned as Southern Baptist torah, was that the light of *oughts* themselves could keep me from the confession and repentance I needed. That is, when I expended all my spiritual energy in living up to rules of my childhood, then I was paradoxically protected from a good, long look in the mirror at how I was actually living as a Christian. I was always trying to get to an imposed, exterior ideal, rather than to a serious consideration of my interior, spiritual life in prayer and my actual behavior as a disciple.

Sometimes repentance is private. That is, issues for confession involve how we are falling short in our seeking and inviting of God's presence in our daily lives. This often involves what are called the sins of *omission*, what we have left undone.

Sometimes repentance is a matter of apology in person when the sin is one of *commission* or movement against another in hurt or anger. And the more power we have in any relationship or group, the greater the risk of such violation of the selfhood of others and the greater our need for the habit of repentance.

Pride always gets in the way. The ego formed in response to others' expectations doesn't ever want to admit that we have fallen short. But to refuse repentance is to carry the albatross of guilt forever. And that is a heavy burden.

Guided Prayer

Dear God,

I am uncomfortable with the spiritual discipline of repentance. Most of the time I deny my need for examination of and reflection on my thoughts, motives, and behavior.

This day I need to turn away from my tendency to _____

_____

_____.

I need to turn back to your grace and mercy because _____

_____

_____.

The sin of omission I need to confess is _____

_____

_____.

The sin of commission I need to confess is _____

_____

_____.

Please infuse my spirit with courage to take the action I need to

take about _____

_____

May your Spirit move within me to bring a change of heart

regarding _____

_____.

Teach me the right order of my days because I seek to live as a person of faithful witness to your love and grace poured out in the world. Amen.

BETRAYAL

Psalm 32

Daily Scripture

* Sunday:

A	B	C
Exodus 17:1-7	Exodus 20:1-17	Isaiah 55:1-9
Psalm 95	Psalm 19	Psalm 63:1-8
Romans 5:1-11	1 Corinthians 1:18-25	1 Corinthians 10:1-13
John 4:5-42	John 2:13-22	Luke 13:1-9

* Monday:	Jeremiah 2:11-13
* Tuesday:	Lamentations 3:37-41
* Wednesday:	Mark 14:10-21
* Thursday:	Matthew 26:14-25
* Friday:	Luke 22:47-54
* Saturday:	Galatians 2:15-21

Meditation

The story of Gethsemane begins in Judas' betrayal of Jesus. Judas, who has been called an "apostle," has turned away. He has become apostate and no longer believes in the gospel which Jesus proclaims, so he betrays Jesus to the religious authorities.

One day during Lenten prayer, the phrase, "if I forget thee, O God," came to my lips unbidden. That phrase has become the symbol to me of my little apostasies. For we tend to consider apostasy as an absolute; that is, we are either believers or not. We are either in a state of belief or of apostasy. This definition assumes faith to be a belief in a set of doctrines to which we either give willed assent or not. And spiritually, such absolutizing can eliminate awareness of our need for daily confession of our daily little apostasies.

But faith is really about how we live, not what we say we believe.

I think the closer truth of a lived-out faith is to acknowledge that we are all apostate at moments in our lives as Christians. We need to acknowledge and confess our daily forgetfulness of God. We all leave God behind in our agendas, schedules, calendars, and human responsibilities. Instead of being still, knowing and waiting for God, we are often out-running God, planning, strategizing, doing and doing and doing.

And it is those unacknowledged, unconfessed daily apostasies that add up, accumulate into a large emptiness and yawning maw of need in our spiritual lives. Often, in those periods of spiritual dryness, we assert that we feel abandoned by God. Perhaps we need to consider that in our daily forgetfulness of God, we are the ones doing the abandoning of relationship and communion.

There is another kind of abandonment that occurs in daily apostasies. When we leave communion with God behind in our days, we also ignore the image of Christ in ourselves. We are disconnected from the primary model of our faith for our lives. As Christians in a challenging, often faithless world, we need a daily sense of connection to the spirit of Christ in our lives. Otherwise we are not living the life of faith. We are only inhabiting the desolation of surviving another day.

The Alcoholics Anonymous phrase, "one day at a time" has significance beyond that recovery process. For, in fact, we all quite literally only have, only get one day at a time. When we wake up each morning, we have been given the gift of a new day. We have been given the gift of a chance to start over in the places in our lives where starting over is required.

And we are given one new day at a time to remember the Lord, our God. We are given one new day at a time to live out our faith as persons formed spiritually by the gospel of Jesus, living out each day as persons imbued by the image of Christ.

Guided Prayer

O my God,

I have been fussing and fretting about too many things, and I have forgotten the one thing that is necessary: to seek you with all my heart and soul and mind.

Recently, I have left you behind by _____

_____

_____

_____.

I have forgotten to seek your presence in my life because _____

_____

_____

_____.

I need to be drawn nearer to your graced and loving holiness so

that _____

_____

_____.

The image of Christ that has been blurred in my lived-out faith is

_____

_____

_____.

Thank you for the gift of each new day of life. Strengthen my heart and faith that I might live this day reflecting the face of Jesus to those I meet. Amen.

IN A GARDEN

Psalm 88

Daily Scripture

* Sunday:

A	B	C
1 Samuel 16:1-13	Numbers 21:4-9	Joshua 9:9-12
Psalm 23	Psalm 107:1-3, 17-22	Psalm 32
Ephesians 5:8-14	Ephesians 2:1-10	2 Corinthians 5:16-21
John 9:1-13, 28-38	John 3:14-21	Luke 15:1-3, 11-32

* Monday:	Mark 14:32-42
* Tuesday:	Job 17:1-16
* Wednesday:	Amos 5:16-24
* Thursday:	1 John 2:7-11
* Friday:	John 1:1-5
* Saturday:	Psalm 139:1-12

Meditation

The story of the garden of Gethsemane takes place in darkness. Jesus, as is his custom, has gone away to pray on the night of his betrayal. The disciples go with him, and he asks only that they stay awake while he prays. This night is the night of Jesus' greatest spiritual struggle. He expects that he will face death, and he prays to be able to accept what is ahead of him.

The disciples fail at their appointed task. Perhaps they are worn out from days of travel and the regular consternation about what exactly their mission is in following Jesus from place to place. The three years have not been easy, and now the teacher they left everything to follow tells them he is going to leave them behind. The disciples nap while Jesus is left alone.

One of the most painful human experiences is to find ourselves in an emotional or spiritual struggle and to feel totally alone in that struggle. Most of us, at one time or another, have "little *g*" gethsemanes in our lives. And to the extent that we find ourselves alone in them, those times in a dark garden do not feel little at all.

One of the themes in spiritual writings about Lent is that now is the time in our Christian life to consider what our struggles with God in a dark time mean to our faith. How do we maintain a living faith when struggles and spiritual darkness threaten to overwhelm the stability of our faith?

Jesus' prayers in the garden reveal that he was not, of course, truly alone. God was present and Jesus was in communion with God. But that communion itself was difficult. Jesus was contending with God about his immediate future. What was going to happen to him? Would it be unbearably painful?

What do we do when even the presence of God in our lives is not that of spiritual comforter? The answer to such a question reflects another theme of the Lenten season. That theme is spiritual growth through and beyond painful and difficult struggles.

A very powerful line in Emily Dickinson's poetry is "Power is only Pain stranded through discipline." That is a summary statement of hundreds of years of spiritual wisdom about what we are to learn about struggle and pain. For struggle and pain are teachers. They teach us about what is crucially important to us. They teach us about what we need to relinquish in order to find more freedom in our faith and to grow as mature Christians. They teach us about our ego's influence on our spiritual life. But more than anything else, struggle and pain teach us to seek God.

One day while walking, I listened to a tape of the theme music from the film *Chariots of Fire*. There is a bass theme that moves in and out slowly beneath the melody. Like the ocean, it ebbs and flows. The image it presented to me was one of God's presence in our lives. For if God's beneficent comfort is present in all our waking moments, we are likely to come to take it for granted as a birthright. The ebbing of God's comfort is what draws us to continue seeking, to continuing praying fervently just as Jesus did in the garden.

The lesson of the garden is learning to stay with the struggle, just as mothers in labor learn to stay with the process of their bodies giving birth. And in that struggle, in the dark times of our lives, we usually find newborn aspects of a deeper and ever more vibrant faith.

Guided Prayer

O my God,

The unknown of my future is like darkness, and I am afraid of darkness. My greatest spiritual struggle in this Lenten season is _____

_____

_____.

The arena of my life that is like a "little *g*" gethsemane is _____

_____

_____.

The pain of that is _____

_____

_____.

Do not draw away your comfort from me. From this pain and

struggle I want to learn _____

_____

_____.

My faith needs renewal because _____

_____

_____.

I seek your face, O God. Come be near and listen to my sighs too deep for tears. Amen.

LAMENTATION

Psalm 38

Daily Scripture

* Sunday:

A	B	C
Ezekiel 37:1-14	Jeremiah 31:31-34	Isaiah 43:16-21
Psalm 130	Psalm 51:1-12	Psalm 126
Romans 8:6-11	Hebrews 5:5-10	Philippians 3:4b-14
John 11:1-45	John 12:20-33	John 12:1-8

* Monday:	Mark 5:25-37
* Tuesday:	Luke 23:26-31
* Wednesday:	Jeremiah 6:16-26
* Thursday:	Psalm 6
* Friday:	Lamentations 3:1-24
* Saturday:	2 Corinthians 1:3-7

Meditation

The word *lamentation* is an old word and not one we hear much in contemporary discourse. The prophets and writers of the Old Testament spoke psalms of lament to God and to the people of Israel, so the Bible recognizes lamentation as a reality for human beings.

During the season of Lent, the cry of lamentation refers to Jesus' cry from the cross recorded in the Gospels of Mark and Matthew. His cry, "My God, my God, why have you forsaken me?" tears at our hearts and insists on the humanity of Jesus with his capacity to be hurt and to feel abandoned. There is no glory here. There is no praise of an omnipotent God. At this point in Jesus' journey, there is no assurance of resurrection for anyone. Jesus expresses the sense of complete forsakenness.

Though Protestants grow up without the tradition of the Stations of the Cross, retreats at Loretto have taught me to pay attention to the images of fourteen events (stations) on the journey Jesus made to Golgotha. The Loretto stations of the cross have a striking feature. Mary, the mother of Jesus, is in all but one of the sculptures. She is a constant and abiding presence in the pain and weariness of that day.

Many Christians also grow up without an image of the *Pietà*. This is the sculpture of Mary holding the body of Jesus after the crucifixion and before burial. Her face is mournful, even resigned, but not despairing. After all, he is flesh of her flesh, bone of her bone.

What are we to make of these contrasting images? While his mother and other women are present, Jesus cries out to God in the pain of forsakenness. The One who has sent him on the mission and ministry of his life seems absent. And the mother who was a disciple has stayed near. Is it possible that we are to see the presence and providence of God in Mary's posture and attentiveness in the *Pietà*?

One of the most basic questions of spiritual formation about the Stations of the Cross is, "Where are we in the picture?" In what aspects of our lives do we make the same journey that Jesus did? Into every Christian life there come what might be termed "little *c*" crucifixions. We carry the burdens of some cross, climb what seem like long, steep hills, and wonder if we will be given over to the forces of oppression in our lives.

Regardless of the final theological meaning of these images of the Stations of the Cross and the *Pietà*, perhaps one of the lessons we should take away from the contrast is the hope that even when we feel abandoned by God, there may be a fellow Christian who can offer comfort.

When we find ourselves with the cry of lamentation on our lips and wrenching our hearts, we should look around. Perhaps there is someone nearer than we might imagine who can hear our cries and offer reassurance.

Knowing of resurrection, we don't have to wait to the end of our journey to find comfort. Believing that all persons are made in the image of God and all Christians have put on Christ, we can seek the encouragement of a brother or sister who offers an understanding heart. On any day of lamentation, we can reach out for the presence of another person who can reflect God's grace to our sore hearts.

Guided Prayer

Dear God,

My lament this season of Lent is about _____

_____

_____.

I sense that I have been forsaken by _____

because _____

_____

_____.

I am oppressed by _____

and I am afraid that _____

_____

_____

_____.

The cry of my heart is _____

_____

_____

_____.

With the psalmist, I trust that you will hear the sound of my weeping and will deliver me by your steadfast love. Please send an emissary of your grace and mercy into my life. Help me to find someone who cares and who can offer comfort and support. Amen.

PALM SUNDAY EXPECTATION

Psalm 96

Daily Scripture

* Sunday:

A	B	C
Isaiah 50:4-9*a*	Isaiah 50:4-9*a*	Isaiah 50:4-9*a*
Psalm 31:9-16	Psalm 31:9-16	Psalm 31:9-16
Philippians 2:5-11	Philippians 2:5-11	Philippians 2:5-11
Matthew 27:11-54	Mark 15:1-39	Luke 23:1-49

* Monday:	John 12:12-19
* Tuesday:	Mark 14:3-9
* Wednesday:	Matthew 26:14-25
* Thursday:	John 13:1-14
* Friday:	Mark 14:32-42
* Saturday:	Mark 15:16-39

Meditation

What a parade it must have been! Jesus rode into Jerusalem in high honor, his presence and intentions celebrated by the people around him. The signs of honor were getting a ride on the back of a donkey, and cloaks and palm branches were laid in front of him as he progressed through the city gates.

But the ride was full of portent. As he was hailed as Messiah by the people who crowded near for a view, others were planning a very different outcome for this man. Jesus' presence, his teaching, and his ministry constantly threatened the status quo. And those in charge of keeping the peace knew the people would have to be persuaded that he was not the deliverer they wanted.

Do you ever wonder what was actually in the mind and heart of Jesus during this ride? He must have known that the lauds and honors would be short-lived; but even so, he was to convey a symbolic message as Messiah in the very act of riding into Jerusalem.

We are more like those folks along the road than we like to admit. As the teenage girl sings in the song, "I want a hero." And much of the time we are searching for a guru who, after we have climbed up the mountain, will give us an answer once and for all to our crucial questions.

If we pay attention to the themes and images of the gospel, we will notice that Jesus and his followers were usually on the road. They were on a journey of ministry, asking questions and growing faith and even doubting now and then all along the way.

Perhaps one of the most helpful symbols of our faith development is that it is a journey toward a deepening, growing, vibrant, and serene faith. There is no substitute for the ongoing faith adventure in the experiences of prayer, worship, Bible study, and Christian community.

As Christians, we follow an itinerant preacher and teacher who went about healing and transforming people's lives by drawing them closer to God. That is what the faith journey is about. For all of us, there is healing that needs to be done, whether it is emotional wounds or spiritual trauma or theological truncation. As Christians, our very lives proclaim the gospel, so the important question becomes, "What are we preaching with our lives?" We pass on our faith to others in community and in the world hoping that the "evangel" will transform their lives.

Perhaps we too need to be cautious if folks want to offer palm branches and cloaks before us. As we walk through Passion week, we must remember to be humbled about what lies at the end of a parade about human glory.

Guided Prayer

Dear God,

I confess my tendency to wish for spiritual rescue. Right now I need to be rescued from _____

_____

_____.

This journey of faith is so hard sometimes, and I am tempted to give over the responsibility for it to someone who seems to have the answers.

What I need in my journey of faith today is _____

_____

_____.

Lead me to the spiritual source for _____

_____

_____.

Draw me closer to you in Christ so that _____

_____

_____.

Make every day of my life a proclamation of your grace and mercy and peace. Amen.

EASTERTIDE

EASTER RESURRECTION

Psalm 118

Daily Scripture

* Sunday:

A	B	C
Acts 10:34-43	Isaiah 25:6-9	Acts 10:34-43
Psalm 118:1-2, 14-24	Psalm 118:1-2, 14-24	Psalm 118:1-2, 14-24
Colossians 3:1-4	Acts 10:34-43	1 Corinthians 15:19-26
John 20:1-18	Mark 16:1-8	John 20:1-18

* Monday:	John 20:1-18
* Tuesday:	Luke 24:1-12
* Wednesday:	Matthew 28:1-10
* Thursday:	Luke 24:13-27
* Friday:	John 20:19-29
* Saturday:	John 21:4-14

Meditation

The harsh winter had turned a Peace climber rose at the corner of our porch totally black. The only thing to be done was cut back all the dead limbs and wait for the rose to grow again from its roots, or not. I fully expected to have to dig up a rose which had long been a favorite.

So on a sunny Good Friday after a Holy Week that had been full of stress and pain, I began clipping the dead branches. It was a day to deal with thorns, but somehow the process was purging. I was clipping off what was only dry sticks and had no chance of rebirth. I would dispose of it, and there would not be a daily reminder of death and loss.

I got down to the crown of the rosebush and brushed away mulch and dead grass to let the light and air of spring in, in hopes that there might be new growth someday.

And there, just beginning to grow toward the sun, were three new short, green canes. They were only inches long, and the red-edged leaves were just beginning to unfurl from both the canes and the crown itself. I rejoiced and thanked God out loud, probably looking fairly silly to any neighbors who might have noticed a middle-aged woman celebrating an early resurrection in her own front yard.

That experience has become an icon for me of what resurrection really means in our life of faith. For just as the disciples had, in despair, given up on Jesus, I had given up on that rosebush. The lesson for me was that resurrection does not depend on my realistic expectations. Or least of all on my own effort.

Resurrection just happens. Resurrection comes into our lives unbidden most of the time just as we have given up hope of new life in the face of some kind of death. There is nothing we can do to *create* resurrection or to make it happen. But, perhaps, there are faith practices that allow us to *make room for* resurrection to happen in our lives.

For I did have to cut the old, dead canes away. The energy that the new canes needed for growth required that. The air and space and light that new leaves need required that.

We naturally dread the experience of grief. But among the important questions for the growth of faith are these: What are we clinging to that is no longer alive for us? What do we need to purge from our spiritual habits, from our prayer life, from a convoluted or destructive relationship? What needs to be clearly and finally mourned so that there will be room in our hearts for resurrection?

In John's Gospel, Mary Magdalene was so shocked by Jesus that she did not recognize him. Barely a day into her grief process over losing him, she was unable to perceive the resurrection there before her eyes.

When the crucifixion and dark days overwhelm our openness to Easter, perhaps we need to consider what we need to prune away in order to make room for resurrection to break in.

Guided Prayer

O God,

I am a creature of habit, even in spiritual matters. What feels no longer alive in my life is _____

_____

_____.

What have I become dependent on in my faith, which needs to be pruned to make room for the new life of resurrection?

_____

_____

The loss or grief which blinds me to Easter rejoicing is _____

_____

_____.

Like Mary Magdalene, I do not know if I would recognize my risen Savior. Heal this pain, O God.
In my life, I need the resurrection of _____

_____

_____.

Renew a right spirit within me, O God, that I may be witness to Resurrection life. Amen.

BLOSSOMING

Psalm 104

Daily Scripture

* Sunday:

A	B	C
Acts 2:14*a*, 22-32	Acts 4:32-35	Acts 5:27-32
Psalm 16	Psalm 133	Psalm 118:14-29
1 Peter 1:3-9	1 John 1:1–2:2	Revelation 1:4-8
John 20:19-31	John 20:19-31	John 20:19-31

* Monday:	Genesis 1
* Tuesday:	Isaiah 35
* Wednesday:	Isaiah 55:6-13
* Thursday:	Ezekiel 34:25-31
* Friday:	Matthew 6:25-33
* Saturday:	John 15:1-11

Meditation

There is something both gentle and luminous about the earth in spring sunshine after an afternoon rain. Mallards splash in puddles with a *pfflump*. Raindrops still cling to grass, and cedar offers its scent. A wine-colored shrub glows in the descending light. White clouds are spackled flat against a suddenly blue sky. Geranium buds in pots are furled, awaiting days of sun.

After a leaden day, time spent in such an environment soothes my spirit in peaceful awe. It is easy to believe that faith and vocation might blossom just beyond a time of transition and confusion.

Because of the usual proximity of Easter and springtime, each adds to the other's significance. They are both about new life. And they are both about promise.

People who are committed gardeners have an intimate connection to the earth and its promise of new life in springtime. Whether it is vegetables and fruits for food or flowers for beauty, gardeners work and plant and watch the blossoming of promise every spring.

Those persons who are committed to lifelong learning also know that blossoming is not something limited to the younger years. A wonderful aspect of our humanity is our ongoing capacity to grow and change. We always have the potential to blossom in a new way.

Midlife is often a time of spiritual search because many of the tasks of adulthood are complete or well on their way. Time spent reflecting on one's journey of faith and one's life can bring whole new vistas of spiritual experience and hope for personal growth in faith and witness.

For the most part, the blossoming of faith or new spiritual depth takes place slowly. Often such growth happens just after a big storm in some area of our life. Just as there are "little *g*" gethsemanes in our lives as Christians, there can also be "little *r*" resurrections. Just when we have given up hope about rejuvenation in our faith or heart, we may discover a capacity for compassion or love or service that we had not ever imagined before.

Wendell Berry has written a poem that ends with the line, "Practice resurrection." The message is simple: Renewal in our faith or life requires practice in order to be brought to fullness. Just as gardeners must be attentive and disciplined to create the conditions for blossoming and fruition, we must pay attention and reserve time and focused energy for the renewal and growth of our spiritual life in order to know the reality of resurrection.

Guided Prayer

Dear God,

The place in my life where I need the promise of new life is _____

_____

_____.

I want _____

to grow in my life so that _____

_____

_____.

Open a vista of spiritual growth in my faith and witness. I need to

practice resurrection in _____

_____

_____.

Show me the place in my life where I need to "plant" my time and energy and blossom into fruition in Jesus' name. Amen.

MERCY

Psalm 103

Daily Scripture

* Sunday:

A	B	C
Acts 2:14*a*, 36-41	Acts 3:12-19	Acts 9:1-20
Psalm 116:1-4, 12-19	Psalm 4	Psalm 30
1 Peter 1:17-23	1 John 3:1-7	Revelation 5:11-14
Luke 24:13-35	Luke 24:36*b*-48	John 21:1-19

* Monday:	Deuteronomy 4:29-31
* Tuesday:	Psalm 131
* Wednesday:	Matthew 9:10-13
* Thursday:	Luke 1:46-55
* Friday:	Luke 10:25-37
* Saturday:	James 3:13-18

Meditation

Many of us walk around, sometimes through our entire life as Christians, without an experiential definition of the spiritual quality of mercy. That is, we have read about mercy, we have heard of it, but even if mercy has been offered to us, we have somehow been unable to let it all the way into the depths of our hearts and to know in those depths what mercy is.

In the words of the hymn by Thomas Moore, we are invited to "Come to the mercy seat...here bring your wounded hearts." In biblical tradition, the mercy seat was the covering of the Ark of the Covenant; it was the abiding place of God, where God dwelled for the wandering Israelites.

One day on retreat at Loretto, my eyes were drawn to a small statue of the Madonna and Child. Made of rough terra-cotta, a haloed Christ Child leans back against Mary's breast, his arms spread wide, one knee bent, one eye slightly askance.

Mary's posture is the posture of all good mothers, of our Good Mother. Her head is bent in a gaze of solicitude. One hand is down by her side, open. The other is open just in front of the Christ Child. She is not holding on to him. But she is kneeling, present, bearing his weight against her and ready to catch if he stumbles or enfold if he cries. Her posture is watchful and open—allowing and encouraging the child's movement out into the world.

Of late, it is the image I have had of myself spiritually. Sitting on God's lap, I am ready to get down and go out into the world into something new, though I don't know what it will be. Perhaps this is one of the meanings of "except you become as a little child." Perhaps we are in some ways spiritual toddlers, needing those watchful and loving eyes of a Parent, needing the mercy seat of a lap to return to when we are hurt or threatened.

The spiritual quality of humility is required for us to imagine ourselves as children of God, needing the merciful kindness of God when our hearts and spirits are battered by life. If the quality of God's mercy is elusive, perhaps it is our proud, adult resistance to leaning on and clinging to God that keeps us away.

The next line of the hymn is "earth has no sorrow that heaven cannot heal." Allowing ourselves to become like a little child with God is the means of finding the healing security of mercy. And in the lap of God, leaning into the kind watchfulness of God's love, we will find mercy.

Guided Prayer

O God,

I do not know whether I want to be vulnerable enough to need your mercy. I am afraid to depend that much on you because _____

_____

_____.

Becoming like a little child again is threatening since _____

_____

_____.

But I do need mercy. I am in need of mercy for _____

_____

_____.

I need your loving watchful gaze upon the _____ in my life. Teach me how to seek the mercy I need. Grant me the humility of a child seeking a loving parent. Amen.

GRACE

Psalm 27

Daily Scripture

* Sunday:

A	B	C
Acts 2:42-47	Acts 4:5-12	Acts 9:36-43, 26-33
Psalm 23	Psalm 23	Psalm 23
1 Peter 2:19-25	1 John 3:6-24	Revelation 7:9-17
John 10:1-10	John 10:11-18	John 10:22-30

* Monday:	Isaiah 30:15, 18-31
* Tuesday:	Joel 2:12-13
* Wednesday:	John 1:1-5, 14-18
* Thursday:	Romans 5:15-17
* Friday:	Ephesians 2:1-10
* Saturday:	1 Peter 4:7-11

Meditation

While we were setting the table for her seventieth birthday dinner, my mother turned to me and asked, "Mary, what is grace?" It was not a facetious question. After spending her entire life busily helping in Methodist and Baptist churches, my mother did not have an experiential definition of grace.

Providentially for the next generation, my sisters and I have found in some arena or another the active sense that grace is available to us as human beings and that it breaks into our lives in the ways and at the times that we need grace. For me, prayer has been a major venue of that inbreaking of grace in the form of insights or revelation about who I am as a beloved creation of God.

The experience of grace falling into our lives, of being washed by God's grace has an immeasurable impact on our self-worth. To experience grace and name it as such is to know ourselves as graced persons. To acknowledge that God has graced us is to recognize that we are blessed.

Matthew Fox has written of the concept of "original blessing" as an antidote to the spiritual misery created by the church's historical emphasis on "original sin." To experience ourselves as originally blessed is to acknowledge that as a unique, individualized creation of God, we are, each one of us, made in the image of God.

God's creation of each of us is God's affirmation of our uniqueness as individuals. That we live and move and have our being is God's determination of our individual human worth. Every new day of our life—every breath—is reaffirmation that God desired that each of us should come to be and that God desires that we should still live.

To truly and deeply accept our original blessing, our being made in the image of God, is to stand open to all the grace that God hopes to pour into our individual life and endeavor. For we can, and often do, stand with our backs to God's grace, stubbornly insisting on our own way.

This is part of the heritage of the theology of original sin. It has often led to what is called works righteousness, or the sense that we must perform as Christians in order to merit grace. But grace can never be merited. Grace can only be accepted as gift, as the wondrous beneficence of God.

When we accept and receive grace, we move toward the enhanced growth and development of our own unique self as a creation. Prayer in the state of received grace is first the prayer of gratitude. But it is also the petition that our life lived, both in prayer and out in the world, will be a life ever more conformed to the particular image of God that we were born to be. The more that happens, the more likely we are to be able to share the grace that we have been given.

Guided Prayer

Dear God,

To stop striving, to depend on your grace is a scary prospect. I wish to know more about my original blessing because _____

_____

_____.

The area of my life where I need the affirmation of being made in your image is _____

_____

_____.

I want to believe that you have determined my worth as _____

_____

_____.

The grace I need right now is _____

_____

_____.

Make me an instrument of your grace in _____

_____

_____.

In the name of Jesus, Amen.

ABUNDANCE

Psalm 145

Daily Scripture

* Sunday:

A	B	C
Acts 7:55-60	Acts 8:26-40	Acts 11:1-18
Psalm 31:1-5, 15-16	Psalm 22:25-31	Psalm 148
1 Peter 2:2-10	1 John 4:7-21	Revelation 21:1-6
John 14:1-14	John 15:1-8	John 13:31-35

* Monday:	Deuteronomy 30:1-10
* Tuesday:	Isaiah 33:2-6
* Wednesday:	Psalm 148
* Thursday:	Matthew 14:13-21
* Friday:	John 10:1-10
* Saturday:	2 Corinthians 9:6-15

Meditation

Nature is the best teacher about developing a sense of abundance in our lives. In her book, *Pilgrim at Tinker Creek,* Annie Dillard celebrates what she calls the fecundity of nature. That is, nature always produces abundantly more seeds and eggs than is necessary for the survival of any species of plant or animal.

If there is one commodity that busy Christians feel like they need in their lives, it is time. And nature's way of beginning and ending the day teaches us about the abundance of time. For in nature the day begins very slowly; light in the east is faint and gradually increases as the earth turns on its axis. The falling of night is a reverse of the morning's movement. There is constant change, but the change itself happens very slowly. Perhaps the development of patience and stillness is necessary to experience abundance.

Nature also teaches that variety and difference are part of abundance. One time on a walk down the front road of Loretto, I noticed for the first time that the sound of wind is different in each tree. In pine trees, it is more like a low, tuneless whistle. In a tulip poplar full of new leaves, the sound is a shush-shushing comforting presence. Perhaps to know abundance we have to be open to variety and difference, to all the possible ways that grace breaks into our lives.

The lake in the back of Loretto is one of my favorite places because it is ringed by woods on three sides. Sitting beside a still body of water is calming to a spirit wearied by the chores of the city. And regardless of sun or the shadow of clouds, the play of light on water teaches me abundance. If the sun shines and the wind blows the lake surface into shallow ripples, the whole lake turns into a field of twinkling, luminous light. If there are clouds, then the color is a shimmering silver. Either kind of light is abundance for the mass of the lake turns with the light.

One day sitting on the porch to rock in the evening, I noticed sunlight gleaming *through* the petals of a red geranium blossom. The combination of light and small flower turned into a glowing carmine, reminiscent of cathedral stained glass windows. And the thought that struck me was that every single day when the sun is at that angle, the beauty of the light shining through red petals happens whether any human being is there to see and appreciate it or not.

The natural world is full of abundance. Scripture is full of abundance. God offers an abundance of life to us. Jesus came to offer life and life more abundantly to all of us.

Guided Prayer

Dear God,

Most of the time, I feel like I don't have enough of something that I need in my life. I don't often consider where there is abundance of your good gifts.

Today I would thank you for the abundance of _____ in my life. You have given me _____ abundantly in my life and I am grateful.

Open my heart to the abundance you offer each day of my life. I need to seek and find and savor an abundance of _____

_____

_____

_____ right now in my life.

With a grateful heart, Amen.

WORSHIP

Psalm 33

Daily Scripture

* Sunday:

A	B	C
Acts 17:22-31	Acts 10:44-48	Acts 16:9-15, 22-29
Psalm 66:8-20	Psalm 98	Psalm 67
1 Peter 3:13-22	1 John 5:1-6	Revelation 21:10–22:5
John 14:15-21	John 15:9-17	John 14:23-29

* Monday: Exodus 20:1-6
* Tuesday: Deuteronomy 10:12-22
* Wednesday: Isaiah 55
* Thursday: Job 38:1-40:1
* Friday: Matthew 4:1-11
* Saturday: John 4:7-26

Meditation

If we have grown up in the church, we tend to believe that we know what worship is. Worship is what happens in church on Sunday mornings when everyone is gathered in the sanctuary.

That is how humans have organized worship. Sometimes what happens in those places at those times is true worship. Sometimes it is not.

Worship as a spiritual reality is more basic. To worship is to honor, glorify, adore, and praise God as Creator, Redeemer, and Sustainer of our lives. Thus worship can happen at any time and in any place. Worship makes our hearts and souls soar with awe and reverence and gratitude. The human organization of worship services aspires to this goal by providing music, prayer, Scripture, proclamation, and communion. The church where I have worshiped for more than twenty-five years formed a tradition of corporate silence before the pastoral prayer. We were communally invited to silence in the midst of public worship. The experience of silence falling in a beautiful room dedicated to the worship of God became one of my favorite parts of the worship service (though I felt some guilt admitting this to ministers who had spent hours and energy on the other elements of worship).

But what the silence did in corporate worship was give explicit recognition that we all were given space and time and silence to invite the presence of God into our own individual worship. Our invitation to silence also created the expectation that we were to specifically seek God in each worship service.

Sometimes corporate worship gets caught up in its own production. Sometimes what we call worship can tend to display human talents. Sometimes worship is so casual that the sense we have is of a family picnic, and there is little expectation that the presence of God will actually be manifest to us.

Worship, whether public or private, is to be focused on God, not on human capabilities. Thus sometimes our most significant experiences of worship occur in private when we humbly acknowledge our need for God's presence, grace, and love.

God calls each of us into presence and communion through the Holy Spirit. When we respond with our whole heart, we are experiencing worship.

Guided Prayer

Dear God,

I need to worship you. I need to be called out beyond the daily concerns of my life to praise and reverence of your creation, power, and grace in the world.

What is missing for me right now in corporate worship is _____

_____

_____.

I need to find _____

_____

_____

in my worship experience.

What worship do you require, O God? What needs to change in my devotional practice so that I find worshipful communion with you?

Teach me your ways, O God. Amen.

ASCENSION SUNDAY

Psalm 97

Daily Scripture

* Sunday:

A	B	C
Acts 1:6-14	Acts 1:15-17, 21-26	Acts 16:16-34
Psalm 68:1-10, 32-35	Psalm 1	Psalm 97
1 Peter 4:12-14; 5:6-11	1 John 5:9-13	Revelation 22:12-14,
John 17:1-11	John 17:6-19	16-17, 20-21
		John 17:20-26

* Monday:	Luke 24:36-52
* Tuesday:	John 16:16-24
* Wednesday:	John 14:1-7
* Thursday:	John 14:18-31
* Friday:	Acts 1:1-14
* Saturday:	Romans 6:3-11

Meditation

The ascension of Jesus into heaven is seen as a celebration by the church, but do you ever wonder whether the disciples were truly happy for him? After all, heavenly glory for Jesus meant absence for them.

The disciples now had their witness and testimony of Jesus' teaching, the Crucifixion and the Resurrection; and they founded Christianity on that good news. They became evangelists—those who tell the story. But Jesus had gone on; the person they shared meals, conversation, travels, and laughter with was no longer with them.

One day I left what was surely the last farewell lunch for one more former colleague and friend from Southern Seminary, which had quickly imploded into fundamentalism. This friend and others were able to go to new places of service and were grateful and excited. But saying farewell did not ever get any easier, no matter our good wishes and shared happiness.

Today such grief is seen as a process that has various elements that we all go through when we experience loss, whether by death or change. Historically, Christians celebrated the entrance into the eternal rest of heaven for anyone who died. But sometimes that covered up the honest sorrow at missing a friend or beloved. When the friendship or love has been life-enhancing, the loss is all the more acute.

Grief counselors teach the importance of being able to say good-bye. But sometimes we miss out on that step. And missing that closure, with the human intimacy it requires, can haunt and tug at our hearts.

One friend died a lingering death from cancer, and I missed the funeral because of an out-of-town trip. Four months later I went to the cemetery. I needed to say what was silenced when my courage failed me, and I stood on frozen ground in the winter chill to speak my regrets out loud. Despite the one-way conversation, finally getting to say good-bye relieved the large stone of grief that had taken up residence in my heart.

Etty Hillesum says, "Give your sorrow all the space and shelter in yourself that is its due, for if everyone hears grief honestly and courageously, the sorrow that now fills the world will abate."

Perhaps it is human nature to resist making time and space in our lives for sorrow and grief. But they are a testament to the meaning and significance in our lives of the one we have lost.

Guided Prayer

O God,

   I miss _____
so much.

   The loss and absence of _____
in my life right now sometimes seems almost more than I can bear.

   The sorrow in my heart is about _____

_____

_____.
God, it hurts so much. I wish I just didn't have to feel this pain.

   I need your comfort and nurture of my sore spirit and heart,
O God. Please wash me with mercy so that I might mourn and then
know renewed gladness. Amen.

PENTECOST

PENTECOST

Psalm 63

Daily Scripture

* Sunday:

A	B	C
Acts 2:1-21	Ezekiel 37:1-14	Acts 2:1-21
Psalm 104:24-34, 35*b*	Psalm 104:24-34, 35*b*	Psalm 104:24-34, 35*b*
1 Corinthians 12:3*b*-13	Romans 8:22-27	Romans 8:14-17
John 20:19-23	John 15:26-27, 16:4*b*-15	John 14:8-17, 25-27

* Monday:	Acts 2:1-21
* Tuesday:	Luke 1:39-45, 68-79
* Wednesday:	Luke 4:14-21
* Thursday:	Romans 8:1-11
* Friday:	1 Corinthians 2
* Saturday:	Galatians 5:22–6:10

Meditation

The season of Pentecost may be the Christian season that receives the least attention by Christians. That is not unusual since it celebrates the coming of the Holy Spirit to inspire the church, and the Holy Spirit is the aspect of the Trinity that has received the least attention in the history of the church and in religious writing.

The Holy Spirit is the mediator of the presence of God in Christian prayer and worship. Few Christians have been taught either Scripture or theology of the Holy Spirit, and even though more and more Christians are beginning a serious spiritual journey and search, there is little material on exactly how one interprets the presence and leading of the Holy Spirit.

As humans strongly influenced by scientific methodology, we are uncomfortable with reality that cannot be empirical. The closest purely human experience to the presence of the Holy Spirit is probably that of intuition or hunches that come to us unbidden as we ponder a problem or situation.

The presence of the Holy Spirit may be sought in a variety of ways. The primary way is prayer. Another is meditation on Scripture or devotional writings. Another is contemplation of nature, music, and art. All these experiences are what are called numinous; that is, we can only describe our perception of them. We cannot "prove" anything about them. We can only testify.

The early Christians in Jerusalem testified of their communal experience of the Holy Spirit at Pentecost. Their description of what happened makes most contemporary Christians very nervous. We don't want flames dancing on our heads, thanks anyway. We don't want to break out speaking in various languages even if that means that we can testify to the presence of God as a result.

Both the Hebrew people in their prophecy and early Christians in their testimony were describing the process of inspiration—of being filled with the Holy Spirit and called by God to speak of that experience. In Hebrew, the word for *breath* and *spirit* are the same. Thus to be inspired of God is to have symbolically breathed in the prophecy, word, judgment, or promise of God. That inspiration is then breathed out when we share it with others.

This sounds like borderline "out of body" or "out of our heads" to modern Americans. We will often choose to live without the presence of God through the Holy Spirit in our lives just as long as we are able to maintain control. But the problem is that then we are choosing to live without inspiration. We are choosing to live without the sense that God through the Holy Spirit is a daily companion, ready to bless our hearts with love and grace, and ready to nourish our faith through inspiration.

That seems a high price to pay to maintain the illusion that, as rational human beings, we are really the ones in control of our lives.

Guided Prayer

Dear God,

I do not know whether I want to be vulnerable to your inspiration or not, God. I am fearful of the change and risk that truly opening to your Spirit might bring.

The part of my life and faith that needs inbreathing of your Spirit

is _____

_____

_____.

I particularly need to feel your presence when _____

_____

_____.

Will you come anew this day into my life? Will you be my daily companion? Breathe on me. Breathe within me. Breathe through me. Amen.

TRINITY SUNDAY

Psalm 19

Daily Scripture

* Sunday:

A	B	C
Genesis 1:1–2:4*a*	Isaiah 6:1-8	Proverbs 8:1-4, 22-31
Psalm 8	Psalm 29	Psalm 8
2 Corinthians 13:11-13	Romans 8:12-17	Romans 5:1-5
Matthew 28:16-20	John 3:1-17	John 16:12-15

* Monday:	Genesis 2:4-25
* Tuesday:	Isaiah 54:4-10
* Wednesday:	John 6:35-40
* Thursday:	John 12:44-50
* Friday:	John 14:8-17
* Saturday:	John 16:1-15

Meditation

The concept of the Trinity has caused no end of problems in the history of theology and the church. Part of the problem, of course, is that neither the word itself nor the concept is explicitly outlined in Scripture.

The theological concept of the Trinity is that God, Jesus Christ, and the Holy Spirit are distinct but equal manifestations of the awesome mystery of God in the world. One newer expression used in liturgy of the Trinity is Creator, Redeemer, and Sustainer.

What happens if we apply the connotations of these three descriptive terms to our daily walk as Christians in the world?

Most days, most of us wake up to alarm clocks, turn over, groan and look for the will to get the day started. Our schedules are such that we seldom reflect on the miracle of a gift of a new day in our lives. But here we are, held by gravity on an earth held in orbit in a universe larger than we can imagine. And every day, the earth rotates and sunlight comes to us once again.

In one sense, our lives are re-created every day and we get a new chance each day to be cocreators with God in the making of a day in a life that has been given to us. There is nothing any of us could do to create our bodies, hearts, minds, or spirits. But we are cocreators with God of what happens in each day of our lives by the decisions we make and the people and places where we invest time and energy. God as Creator lives in us and urges us to make a life full of purpose and meaning, lived out in the name of Jesus the Christ.

Jesus is Savior and Redeemer of our lives. The confession of sin and acceptance of Jesus' death on the cross and resurrection is the beginning step in our redemption. However, sin remains a part of our human tendencies. So redemption or salvation is an ongoing process whereby we keep offering up confession and learning forgiveness and living more fully as redeemed persons. As disciples of a Redeemer, we spend our lives by participating in the redemption of others from the pain and losses of their lives. Whether immediately in our vocation or symbolically in our discipleship, we announce good news to the poor, proclaim release for those imprisoned, recover sight for the blind, let the broken victims go free, and proclaim the year of the Lord's favor.

Jesus' teaching about the Holy Spirit was as Comforter, as active presence of the sustaining grace, mercy, peace, and love of God in our lives. The sad truth is that people can spend their whole lives in church and seldom experience this spiritual sustenance. Those who seem to be most closely in touch with the Holy Spirit are persons of prayer, for it is in honest, seeking, regular prayer where we encounter the God who seeks to offer us unceasing abundant life of the spirit.

These are the motions of the Trinity: creation, redemption, and sustenance. They are offered to us every day as a spring of water always welling up. We only have to stop, lay aside the world's priorities, and sit for a while drinking from an overflowing cup.

Guided Prayer

Dear God,

Thank you for the gift of this day in my life. Teach me the humility to name each day a gift and miracle of grace which I offer back to you in service.

I need energy for cocreation today in order to _____

_____

_____.

The sin which has been plaguing me is _____

_____

_____.

I need redemption from _____

_____

_____.

The comfort and sustenance I need from your Holy Spirit is _____

_____

_____.

Distract me, Lord, from all my human distractions that keep me too busy to go to the spring of water always welling up, which is your grace and mercy, peace and love. Amen.

SANCTIFICATION

Psalm 106

Daily Scripture

* Sunday:

A	B	C
Genesis 6:9-22, 7:24, 8:14-19	1 Samuel 3:1-10	1 Kings 8:22-23, 41-43
Psalm 46	Psalm 139:1-6, 13-18	Psalm 96:1-9
Romans 1:16-17, 3:22*b*-28	2 Corinthians 4:5-12	Galatians 1:1-12
Matthew 7:21-29	Mark 2:23–3:6	Luke 7:1-10

* Monday:	Isaiah 29:17-24
* Tuesday:	John 17:1-19
* Wednesday:	Romans 6:17-23
* Thursday:	Hebrews 13:8-16
* Friday:	1 Thessalonians 5:4-24
* Saturday:	1 John 4:7-21

Meditation

Are we supposed to aspire to sainthood in this lifetime? What does this word *sanctification* mean to modern Christians? To *sanctify* is to make holy or sacred. That seems a preposterous, even prideful, goal for Christians. What does it mean to expect that our lives and actions might be made more holy for God?

One good bridge to this idea is the true meaning of sacrifice. The common connotation is that sacrifice means that we give something up for a higher purpose. But the root word actually means offering that is proffered to God in order that God might determine the sacredness of the offering.

In this context, sanctification becomes the ongoing process of offering up our time, energy, and lives to God's purposes. Such offering relinquishes the human determination of whether our growth and development as Christians are toward holiness or sacredness. God makes the determination.

Thus sanctification is closely akin to humility. For as humans, our first tendency is to focus on our own agency or power to make things happen. To make our time, energy, and lives an ongoing offering to God relinquishes some of our human power to decide the outcome of what we do.

Just like other spiritual processes, sanctification is a lifelong endeavor. A central issue in any person's spiritual journey is the discernment of what actions are our responsibility and what decisions are supposed to wait upon further revelation from God. So sanctification means a daily offering of our time, energy, and life to God's intended intervention in the world.

One day in prayer, the unbidden sentence came to thank God for the blessing and gift of each new day of life. And the requisite act in prayer on my part was to offer the day back to God. This impulse in prayer came at a time when there was great vocational and emotional stress in my life. What the gratitude for and relinquishment of the day meant was that I was relieved of the burden of feeling that I must, all by myself, make progress every day on solving some part of the ongoing problems at work and in my personal life.

So my testimony is that sanctification—the offering of our time, energy, and lives into God's providence—may result in the relief of burdens, rather than the loss of personal power.

Guided Prayer

Dear God,

Sanctification seems like such a preposterous goal for the Christian life. Just making growth in discipleship another task for the day is not an easy thing to do.

Today, I would offer up to you _____

_____

_____.

What initiative am I responsible for today? I am burdened about

_____

_____.

Should I wait on your movement?

I want to grow toward offering my life, offering all my days, to the movement and power of your Holy Spirit in the world. Show me how. Amen.

SPIRITUAL GIFTS

Psalm 107

Daily Scripture

* Sunday:

A	B	C
Genesis 12:1-9	1 Samuel 8:4-11, 16-20	1 Kings 17:17-24
Psalm 33:1-12	Psalm 138	Psalm 30
Romans 4:13-25	2 Corinthians 4:13–5:1	Galatians 1:11-24
Matthew 9:9-13, 18-26	Mark 3:20-35	Luke 7:11-17

* Monday:	Matthew 7:7-11
* Tuesday:	Ephesians 4:1-7, 11-13
* Wednesday:	1 Corinthians 12:1-13
* Thursday:	1 Timothy 4:4-16
* Friday:	2 Timothy 1:6-14
* Saturday:	1 Peter 4:7-11

Meditation

Discipleship programs to help Christians discover their spiritual gifts are in vogue these days. The intention of the exploration process is the spiritual empowerment of individual Christians as well as the church, since a living sense of spiritual empowerment is essential to healthy ministry.

What does it mean to be gifted by the Holy Spirit? Is the reality of spiritual empowerment some kind of borderline strange experience that we might not be able to control?

As Genesis 1:28 notes that all human beings are made in the image of God, the premise of spiritual gifts is that each individual Christian's creation is one of the reflected images of God. Thus, to learn and acknowledge, practice and live out of one's spiritual giftedness is to live out of the unique and finite image of God that our individual creation signifies.

The Ephesians 4:7 passage notes that our spiritual gifts are our own portion of "Christ's bounty." *Bounteous* and *bountiful* are derivations of the word that sound old-fashioned to us. But what they mean is "abundant goodness." In Christ, there is more than enough goodness to go around, and the goodness is freely and generously offered to us through the activity of the Holy Spirit in our lives.

The crux of the issue is how we connect spiritually with the activity of the Holy Spirit in our lives so that we are living in partnership and living as Christians out of our spiritual gifts. For spiritual gifts are like any other human capability: having been gifted, we are then responsible for how we bear those gifts and live our Christian life out of those gifts.

For many active Christians, the mere mention of one more responsibility brings a groan of fatigue. But many times we have signed on for a ministry responsibility because we were convinced by a person doing the recruiting that there just wasn't anyone else available.

What living out of a sense of spiritual giftedness means is that we do our ministry not from a sense of deprivation of time and energy and not from a sense of desperation that something important won't get done. Doing our ministry as Christians out of the spiritual empowerment of giftedness means that we live and move and have our being connected to a vibrant sense of the abundant goodness of God.

We don't have to create everything and handle everything and be completely responsible. What we do have to do is stay in daily touch with God's leading in our lives through prayer. Prayer becomes both a form of and the means of ministry done out of our spiritual gifts.

Guided Prayer

Dear God,

    With everything else I have to do, I don't know if I want the responsibility of spiritual gifts. So far, I believe that my gift of the Spirit is _____

_____

_____.

What I do want to give to others in your name is _____

_____

_____.

    I want to live and move and have my being within the movement of your Holy Spirit in the world. Show me how to lean on your grace for the wisdom and energy needed to live as a gifted Christian. Amen.

COMMUNITY OF FAITH

Psalm 84

Daily Scripture

* Sunday:

A	B	C
Genesis 18:1-15	2 Samuel 15:34–16:13	1 Kings 21:1-10,
Psalm 116:1-2,	Psalm 20	15-21*a*
12-19	2 Corinthians 5:6-10,	Psalm 5:1-8
Romans 5:1-8	14-17	Galatians 2:15-21
Matthew 9:35–10:8	Mark 4:26-34	Luke 7:36–8:3

* Monday:	Matthew 10:32-42
* Tuesday:	Matthew 25:31-40
* Wednesday:	Luke 14:12-24
* Thursday:	1 Corinthians 12:13-27
* Friday:	Colossians 1:15-23
* Saturday:	Colossians 3:12-17

Meditation

In the Baptist churches of my childhood Communion, or the Lord's Supper as we called it, was always served by the deacons to the members in the pew. From the first time that I ever went "down front" to receive Communion directly from the hands of a minister, that ritual for Communion has seemed to me the way it really ought to be done.

For there is something about going to get the bread and the cup, rather than having it delivered to me, safely ensconced in the pew, that is a metaphor for how we are to live out our lives together in the church. We are not going to be spoon-fed; neither true Communion with God nor true community with one another is going to be delivered to us while we sit passively waiting.

Communion as a symbol of the church community also has the

important aspect of being available to everyone. The table belongs to Jesus Christ, not to the church, not to the pastor or to the deacons. Thus we are to model in our church community the open hospitality of Jesus as he welcomed, fed, and offered healing to all persons in his presence.

Another image from a Loretto retreat indicates how that hospitality of caring support shows up in the community of faith. One older sister, still in her long, black Loretto habit and bent, almost shrunken, offers her arm to a younger nun who is dressed in contemporary garb. Though the younger woman is larger in frame and not nearly as frail looking as the older sister, she leans on a cane and limps. They are a parable of the shared, needy vulnerability we have as Christians in this life. At one time or another, each one of us, no matter what our strengths and capabilities, needs someone to lean on. Sometimes in shared trauma we need someone to lean with. If we cannot lean on each other out of weakness, we will all fall down by ourselves.

These lessons were hard to learn when the church was a dominant cultural influence. Too often the church has been imbued with levels of social status, both within the church itself and between churches.

Today, the challenges that face each individual community of faith might bring us back to the basics. What our community of faith has to offer that is unique compared to any other kind of community is the overriding issue. We will have to get out of the pew to experience Communion, to receive spiritual nourishment. We are responsible for creating a hospitable welcome to all who would come to join us. And we must recognize that we will at times need to be vulnerable to one another out of the traumas of our lives. Thereby we will discover the strength of God which undergirds our human weakness.

Guided Prayer

Dear God,

Communion sometimes seems like just a ritual, Jesus. Open my heart to its deeper meaning for my discipleship. I would know you

better because _____

_____

_____.

Hospitality is much easier to provide to people who are like me. What persons or group am I supposed to reach out to in hospitality who are now strangers to me?

Right now, I need to lean on the gracious hospitality of another

Christian because _____

_____

_____.

Lead me to such a person.
And when I am able, lead me to the tasks of building up the community of faith. Amen.

FRUITS OF THE SPIRIT

Psalm 1

Daily Scripture

* Sunday:

A	B	C
Genesis 21:8-21	1 Samuel 17:33-49	1 Kings 19:1-4, 8-15*a*
Psalm 86:1-10, 16-17	Psalm 9:9-20	Psalm 42
Romans 6:1*b*-11	2 Corinthians 6:1-13	Galatians 3:23-29
Matthew 10:24-39	Mark 4:35-41	Luke 8:26-39

* Monday:	Galatians 5:22-25
* Tuesday:	Ezekiel 36:24-30
* Wednesday:	Matthew 7:15-20
* Thursday:	John 15:1-17
* Friday:	James 3:13-18
* Saturday:	Romans 8:18-27

Meditation

The actual development of fruit on a tree can be a metaphor for the way that the fruits of the Spirit grow in our faith life as disciples of Jesus Christ. First the sap rises invisibly. Then flowers grow, which are transformed into fruit. And within every piece of fruit there are seeds which, when germinated and nurtured, can grow into other trees. Any gardener who wants to grow fruit successfully knows that certain kinds of care such as fertilizing, spraying, and pruning are necessary for a successful harvest of succulent fruit.

The Galatians passage about the fruits of the Spirit is a list of wondrous qualities that all human beings would want to have in their lives. It is a list of Christian discipleship. The first important consideration is that these qualities of character and personality are fruits of the *Spirit of God;* that means that they are not human creation. Just as we cannot add time to our lifespan, we cannot create these qualities in ourselves.

However, just as we are born with the innate capacity to sin, we are born with the capacity in our hearts, minds, and spirits of receiving the fruits of the Spirit and letting those qualities grow in our lives. The grace of God in giving these fruits of the Spirit to each of us is like a fruit tree's sap rising in the spring.

Grace itself is ephemeral, as invisible to human sight as sap rising. And whether we experience God's grace in our lives depends on the ground where we are planted; it depends on what kind of earth we send our roots into.

Growing Christlike is a matter of becoming ever more open to the fruits of the Spirit in our lives. Too often, the list of qualities is interpreted in our individualistic, achievement-oriented society as realities that we somehow create in ourselves, as one more list of "good person" attributes that we are supposed to achieve.

But first, foremost, and repeatedly, we have to *accept* the fruits of the Spirit as the gifts that they are. We must open our hearts, minds, and spirits to receive love, joy, peace, patience, kindness, goodness, fidelity, gentleness, and self-control. Imagine what life would feel like if we lived our lives believing that God was constantly holding out these fruits of the Spirit as gifts to us. Imagine what our lives together would be like if we lived out of a sense that, in different ways and to different degrees, these fruits of the Spirit were ours to offer to one another on a daily basis.

How do we learn to receive these fruits so that we can then live out of them in our family and church and community? First of all, a humble posture in prayer is required. We have to acknowledge that we are incapable of creating the qualities in ourselves or in the world. We have to empty ourselves of the ego which asserts that we can create them by intention.

We have to recognize that our capacity to receive and live out of these fruits of the Spirit fluctuates from day to day. Thus we have to seek from God in petitionary prayer the gift of the particular fruit that we need each day.

One of the standard truths for mentors and therapists is that they cannot give away what they do not have. This is also true for disciples of Christ. We have to stay connected to the Spirit of Christ so that we can receive the fruits of the Spirit. Then the qualities of love, joy, peace, patience, kindness, goodness, fidelity, gentleness, and self-control come to fruition and we can plant the seeds of them for others.

Guided Prayer

Dear God,

The fruit of the Spirit which has been missing in my life is

_____

_____.

I need the grace of that fruit of the Spirit in my life right now

because _____

_____

_____.

The teaching that you are always and constantly offering these gifts to me is astonishing. How do I stay connected to your presence in the Holy Spirit in order to receive them?

The fruit of the Spirit which I have accepted from you is _____

_____

_____.

Where am I supposed to go in order to share with others? Amen.

DISCIPLESHIP

Psalm 37

Daily Scripture

* Sunday:

A	B	C
Genesis 22:1-14	2 Samuel 1:1, 17-27	2 Kings 2:1-2, 6-14
Psalm 13	Psalm 130	Psalm 77:1-2, 11-20
Romans 6:12-23	2 Corinthians 8:7-15	Galatians 5:1, 13-25
Matthew 10:40-42	Mark 5:21-43	Luke 9:51-62

* Monday:	Luke 9:23-27
* Tuesday:	Matthew 10:5-15
* Wednesday:	Matthew 10:16-23
* Thursday:	Matthew 10:24-42
* Friday:	Mark 10:35-45
* Saturday:	John 21:4-17

Meditation

A number of the Gospel stories featuring the disciples sound a little like the adventures of a troupe of muddle-headed clowns. Jesus was repeatedly having not only to teach, but to interpret and reinterpret his message for them. Perhaps those of us inclined to strict ideals and judgment about what constitutes the Christian life should take comfort that, from the beginning, disciples and their foibles have been very public.

Disciple, after all, means follower; it does not mean perfect righteousness. Following is what the disciples did. They stayed on the journey with Jesus up through the last night. And their hearts were open to his visits with them after the Resurrection.

In "church language" discipleship has come to mean more what we do as Christians than who we are. And in a society geared toward achievement, we risk being overwhelmed by a church or Christian "to do" list.

The language of spiritual gifts teaches us that discipleship is an individual matter. That is, some will teach, some will lead, some will serve according to the gifts and talents of each. And the whole of the witness of the church will then be more than the sum of its parts.

If *disciple* is an identity (who we *are* and not what we *do*), then we live out of our discipleship all the time in all of our roles, not just those at church or in Christian service. And the spiritual formation of a disciple requires regular contact with the teacher.

That means that the spiritual disciplines of the interior life—the journey inward—are just as important as the disciplines of the exterior life—the journey outward. Prayer, solitude, silence, and Scripture are the spiritual nurture of a Christian who takes seriously the mandate to be in the world offering the gospel of Jesus as both word and deed.

A genuine outward journey of discipleship will occasionally try the patience of any saint-in-training. There may be a long stretch of time when no one says, "thank you." Christian service is usually devoid of public glory. We will have to respond to and serve with some folks who have truly quirky personalities. They may believe the same about us and not be reticent about expressing their opinions. After all, no matter the form of discipleship, we will be working with other human beings; and all of us are muddle-headed clowns at one time or another.

The most important feature of Christian discipleship is the particular teacher that we follow. Jesus came into the world and transformed the hearts and lives of the people that he met. No one else will ever be just like Jesus. But if we are students of his way and disciples of his teachings, we will stay in contact with the risen Christ who calls us out to follow and to learn and to serve. We will be in formation, in the process of becoming and being disciples.

Guided Prayer

Dear God,

I would follow Jesus Christ as disciple, but the teaching about losing my life in order to save it is confusing. To listen to Jesus as my teacher, I need to learn more about _____

_____

_____.

The hardest part of being a disciple for me is _____

_____

_____.

My journey inward in prayer needs _____

_____

_____.

My journey outward in service needs to _____

_____

_____.

Teach me, O Christ, your way. Amen.

HUMILITY

Psalm 25

Daily Scripture

* Sunday:

A	B	C
Genesis 24:34-38, 42-49, 58-67	2 Samuel 5:1-5, 9-10	2 Kings 5:1-14
Psalm 45:10-17	Psalm 48	Psalm 30
Romans 7:15-25*a*	2 Corinthians 12:2-10	Galatians 6:7-16
Matthew 11:16-19	Mark 6:1-13	Luke 10:1-11, 16

* Monday:	2 Chronicles 7:12-16
* Tuesday:	Isaiah 57:12-19
* Wednesday:	Zephaniah 2:8-13
* Thursday:	Luke 14:7-14
* Friday:	Philippians 2:1-8
* Saturday:	1 Peter 5:1-11

Meditation

One of the first sights at Loretto is Badin Pond. The intent of the pool is to make its sights and sounds and the pasture surrounding it accessible to those who roll in wheelchairs to get where they are going. There is a soaring sculpture of a crane pointed to the sky and a purple martin house with straggles of straw from a new nest. A covered porch gives mother duck and her bevy of twelve brown and yellow babies a place to rest.

There is a sidewalk surrounding the pond, and it reveals the fund-raising plan for its construction. Inscribed in each poured section is one or more names in no particular order. Many names are of German origin as befits the surrounding community. Many are in memoriam of beloved women dedicated to God. Some are even whimsical.

So anytime anyone treks around the edge of Badin Pond, these persons' names are literally walked on. The folks who donated money and their names for this sidewalk must be very humble. They have written their names to be walked on. They have quite literally inherited the earth along with the constant possibility of humiliation by indiscriminate ducks.

Humility is the most elusive spiritual gift. One of my professors used to say that as soon as a person considered himself or herself humble, the person had lost humility. We cannot ever be proud of our humility.

Some people are naturally humble. They have always lived intrinsically by the current management dictum that there is no limit to what you can accomplish if no one cares who gets the credit. Praise and public recognition just don't stick to these people.

Other people have learned the privilege of service and thereby found humility. For one of the lessons of maturity is the wonder of giving without expecting return. The joy of humility is found in service, whatever kind it is, even service that has significant public power involved.

Only the humble heart can know and experience this joy. For Christians the model of Jesus means that we take risks in order to live out the service we each find to do. Jesus was publicly humiliated when he was run out of his home town. He was humbled when his family considered him unstable and tried to pull him back into the fold.

Since the words, *humility* and *humiliation* have the same root, we need to ponder the possible connection between the two human experiences. Humiliation is not always required in order to have the gift of humility, but perhaps taking the chance of being humiliated is one form of humility.

Chances are few of us will face the humiliation of a public trial, but even there Jesus' posture was a humble one. The model we have is a difficult one to follow. But the method is the same. Jesus was able to carry out his humble service on this earth because he lived and ministered within a constant sense of the presence of God. Seeking to live our lives in that same place offers us the possibility of the gift of humility.

Sometimes life has lessons to teach us through humiliation. The issue then is whether our heart is willing to listen and learn.

Guided Prayer

O God,

I don't know if I value humility as a spiritual gift enough to risk humiliation in order to learn humility. As a Christian, I am most likely

to feel proud of myself when _____

_____

_____.

Humility seems most elusive in my life when _____

_____

_____.

I know humility is not something I can create or attain. The desire to humbly serve you is a gift from you. Soften my heart, that I might truly desire such a gift. Amen.

SERVANTHOOD

Psalm 86

Daily Scripture

* Sunday:

A	B	C
Genesis 25:19-34	2 Samuel 6:1-5, 12*b*-19	Amos 7:7-17
Psalm 119:105-12	Psalm 24	Psalm 82
Romans 8:1-11	Ephesians 1:3-14	Colossians 1:1-14
Matthew 13:1-9, 18-23	Mark 6:14-29	Luke 10:25-37

* Monday:	1 Kings 8:22-30
* Tuesday:	Isaiah 42:1-9
* Wednesday:	Mark 9:33-37
* Thursday:	Luke 7:36-50
* Friday:	Luke 12:32-40
* Saturday:	John 13:3-17

Meditation

There is probably no more threatening image of the Christian life to competent, achievement-oriented Americans than that of the servant. In biblical times, servants were an everyday reality for most people. There was, and of course still is, a basic economic line of demarcation as to whether a person is a servant or has enough economic capital to hire servants to do menial labor. Today, immigrants still see the mode of servanthood as maid, nanny, or gardener as a first step to the American dream.

But the biblical word about servanthood for believers is that it is a voluntary state entered into as a means of living out faith. To be a servant is to be of service to another. Perhaps a primary conundrum for American Christians is the pull between a sense of personal status and the image of servanthood.

The ultimate New Testament image of servanthood is the basin and towel representing one of the last acts of Jesus. After functioning with his disciples as rabbi, teacher, preacher, healer, and Messiah, the last role Jesus fills with his followers is that of servant.

And he performs the most menial job of a servant. In those days, people's feet were daily and regularly dirty from the streets and fields. A primary gesture of hospitality was the offer of a servant who brought fresh water and a towel to wash a guest's feet. The posture of this act is also humbling. Servants would kneel, face and eyes lowered to the task, while the guest sat.

Have you ever had your feet washed? As a child, going barefoot whenever possible in the Oklahoma dust meant sometimes going in to run an inch of water in the tub and just wash my feet before socks and shoes were required. If your feet have ever been hot and dusty, the sensation of cool water washing over them is not forgotten.

The disciples were naturally aghast. Why was their master lowering himself to the posture and gesture of a servant? We have tended to elevate Jesus' divinity over his humanity and would also probably protest just as the disciples did.

But everything that Jesus did was for us too. Being a Christian means learning to receive the mercy, grace, and love of a servant Messiah. And it means following him into the actual and symbolic posture of a servant, basin and towel in hand, kneeling at the feet of weary folks who need our service of mercy and the gift of compassion.

Guided Prayer

Dear God,

I cannot imagine Jesus kneeling before me to wash my feet, just as it is difficult to imagine washing another's feet. I need my public human status in my role as _____

_____

_____

because _____

_____

_____.

What servanthood do you require of me this day? Where is the place and who are the people who need my service?

In the name of a Savior who washed feet, Amen.

FASTING

Psalm 141

Daily Scripture

* Sunday:

A	B	C
Genesis 28:10-19*a*	2 Samuel 7:1-14*a*	Amos 8:1-12
Psalm 139:1-12, 23-24	Psalm 89:20-37	Psalm 52
Romans 8:12-25	Ephesians 2:11-22	Colossians 1:15-28
Matthew 13:24-30, 36-43	Mark 6:30-34, 53-56	Luke 10:38-42

* Monday:	2 Samuel 12:15*b*-23
* Tuesday:	Isaiah 58:2-9
* Wednesday:	Matthew 6:16-18
* Thursday:	Matthew 6:24-33
* Friday:	Mark 2:18-20
* Saturday:	Acts 14:21-23

Meditation

I am a confirmed and unrepentant chocoholic. My easy rationale is that it is such a minor addiction and I am grateful to God for the creation of the cocoa bean. One excursion with a friend resulted in the consumption of a good-sized brownie with a scoop of chocolate ice cream on top. When the waiter asked if I wanted chocolate syrup too, I demurred, noting that the brownie had a thick frosting. But I recognize that, in such a situation, refusing chocolate syrup certainly does not constitute fasting.

Fasting is a biblical tradition focused on spiritual goals. Generally, fasting is seen as a cleansing process for the purpose of seeking revelation from God. In the history of the church, fasting occasionally has been taken to the extremes of self-mortification.

The concept as a spiritual discipline traditionally involves food. To fast is to go without, to do without. But in a contemporary America, bombarded by the commercial messages that consumption of something, almost anything, that might make us happier and more content, we find fasting to be an odd term, consigned to the space behind monastery walls.

One very important question for consumer-oriented Americans is, What is enough? Whether it is money, clothes, prestige, food, power, friends, what is enough? This is a question that a system based in unlimited growth does not want consumers to ask.

But seeking the true, practical definition of *enough* is a crucial spiritual question. For the spiritual life does involve limits on our human wants and desires. And *enough* is an individual definition arrived at through consideration of basic needs and values rather than consumer hype or "keeping up with the Joneses."

One of the lessons of a thoughtful middle age is the awareness that too many possessions often possess us rather than the other way around. Our houses, closets, drawers, and lives are sometimes cluttered with the possessions that at one time seemed crucially needed. The old rule that if you haven't worn it or used it in the last year, you probably don't need it is a good one for increasing simplicity in our lives.

Thus for contemporary American Christians the concept of fasting is a much broader one than just doing without food for a set period of time, even though some occasionally may feel led to such a practice. Fasting is a kind of relinquishment of the too-muchness of our busy and complex lives. Fasting is a simplifying of mind and heart and habits.

"Doing without" is a concept that has almost lost its meaning as the memories of the Great Depression fade from our culture's memory. That generation learned to "do without." The spiritual discipline of fasting is a relearning of the need and benefits of "doing without."

Guided Prayer

Dear God,

Fasting seems like such an old-fashioned idea. What is enough?

I still feel that I need more_____

_____

_____.

But I also feel the burden of too much _____

_____

_____.

From what am I called on to fast this day? What do I let go of in relinquishment? What am I to learn to do without?
In the name of Jesus who lived as a lily in the field, Amen.

WEEK 35

FREEDOM IN CHRIST

Psalm 121

Daily Scripture

* Sunday:

A	B	C
Genesis 29:15-28	2 Samuel 11:1-15	Hosea 1:2-10
Psalm 105:1-11, 45*b*	Psalm 14	Psalm 85
Romans 8:26-39	Ephesians 3:14-21	Colossians 2:6-15
Matthew 13:31-38, 44-52	John 6:1-21	Luke 11:1-13

* Monday:	Galatians 5:1, 13-14
* Tuesday:	Exodus 12:29-51
* Wednesday:	Matthew 11:28-30
* Thursday:	Luke 13:11-17
* Friday:	John 8:31-36
* Saturday:	Romans 6:15-23

Meditation

One of Rollo May's first books outlines the human fear of freedom. For in spite of the American political value of freedom and the culture's emphasis on personal freedom, most human beings fear the emotional and social isolation that is always a risk of such freedom.

When we are free in an arena of our lives, whether it is political, personal, social, or religious, we have a parallel responsibility for how we live in that freedom. The refusal to accept a level of freedom has the handy consequence of then not being held responsible for how we handle that kind of freedom.

What does it mean to live in freedom? How does that feel? What exactly are our fears about freedom?

The Pharisees of Jesus' day did not want freedom for themselves

163

or anyone else. They were very threatened by the message of love and grace that Jesus brought because the Law they upheld did not have those elements in the same way that Jesus exemplified in his preaching and healing. In the face of Roman political and economic oppression, Jewish religious leaders had arrived at the only possible compromise for their people's continued religious expression. But that meant that the jots and tittles of the Law were what became the overriding aspect of their lives. The Pharisees simply could not imagine the spiritual freedom Jesus experienced as the Messiah, so they had to try to control him.

Martin Luther recovered the message of spiritual freedom in the New Testament, and the Reformation was born. For what the freedom of Christ means is that we choose as spiritually free persons created by God whether or not we will follow Jesus. To be free in Christ is to bear the responsibility to keep choosing Christ as teacher, model, and savior.

The message of Reformation teaching about freedom in Christ is that a faith that is not freely chosen by the heart and mind of the believer is really no faith at all. The outer manifestations of faith can be coerced by family expectations or by the social power of a congregation. Some persons find themselves in a crisis of faith when they realize that they have been living on borrowed faith and they do not have one of their own.

Each of the disciples could have said no to Jesus' calling when they heard their names. We too have the freedom to say no to God as the ongoing Creator of our lives and to Christ as the ongoing Redeemer of our lives and to the Holy Spirit as ongoing Sustainer of our faith. It is only within that kind of spiritual freedom that a faith that sustains our lives can grow. And within that realm of spiritual freedom, we bear ongoing responsibility for nourishing our faith and ministering to others.

Guided Prayer

Dear God,

I do not feel free about _____

_____

_____.

Perhaps I am afraid of freedom. If for freedom Christ has set us free, what kind of freedom in my life and faith do I need to seek?

I fear the responsibility of _____

in regard to freedom. But I cherish the freedom to keep choosing faith in Christ, for that is the foundation of my life.

Teach me about your freedom so that I may continue to choose faith. Amen.

ORDINARY TIME

SISTERS AND BROTHERS

Psalm 67

Daily Scripture

* Sunday:

A	B	C
Genesis 32:22-31	2 Samuel 11:26–12:13a	Hosea 11:1-11
Psalm 17:1-7, 15	Psalm 51:1-12	Psalm 107:1-9, 43
Romans 9:1-5	Ephesians 4:1-6	Colossians 3:1-11
Matthew 14:13-21	John 6:24-35	Luke 12:13-21

* Monday:	Matthew 5:21-24
* Tuesday:	Mark 3:31-35
* Wednesday:	John 11:1-44
* Thursday:	Romans 14:10-23
* Friday:	1 John 2:7-11
* Saturday:	1 John 3:11-23

Meditation

The ragtag band of disciples and women who followed Jesus throughout Galilee must have received incredulous looks, rude comments, and maybe caused a camel wreck or two. For these were a group of men and women unrelated by marriage or family who were choosing to be together in order to follow their teacher. They were a walking, talking social revolution within their larger society because male and female roles were narrowly prescribed and enforced by Judaic law.

While I worked at a seminary, one of the preaching professors would greet me in the hall by saying, "Good morning, Sister Zimmer" out of his African American tradition. I loved hearing that because the title of "sister" established symbolically the relationship he and I shared in Christ even though we seldom had any extended conversation. It was a public acknowledgment of our connection in Christ and our equality before God.

I grew up without any biological brothers, and some of God's greatest gifts to me have been brothers-in-law who treat me like a sister. They both tease me and respect me and offer me sturdy affection. Within the crucible of a crisis-ridden seminary, I consciously adopted brothers in ministry and the church. These friendships are sustaining grace in my life.

One of the most important models the church can offer the world is the image of men and women living and working together as Christians who are spiritual and emotional brothers and sisters. Sometimes that kind of intentional extended sibling network can heal old wounds from alienated natural sibling relationships. Sometimes it is just a particular wonder of a human level of intimacy and affection in which sex is forbidden, so we can all just relax.

Being sisters and brothers together in Christ is inherently a model of the egalitarian church. For it is a relationship that is initiated in, grows in, and thrives in the mutual seeking after the image of Christ in our lives. The promise of "where two or three are gathered in my name, there I am also" is what makes brothers and sisters of us. We are together not only as human beings but as conjoint images of Christ in the world.

Such a model of men and women working together in the name of faith and the spiritual life is one of the unique features of the church. No other social structure has that to offer. The mutual sharing of care, support, and compassion is a reality that many people isolated by our hectic, technological world are looking for. When we are honestly and fairly brothers and sisters in the church, then the world will notice and perhaps be curious about how that happens and come in to inquire.

Guided Prayer

Dear God,

Sometimes it is hardest to love those we know best in the church. The most painful betrayal is one Christian to another.

I have been burdened by a conflict or hurt feelings about

_____ with _____.

I need reconciliation with _____

because _____

_____

_____.

I need spiritual connection with brothers and sisters in Christ. Lead me to know the means by which I can find that in my church and learn how to trust others with my deepest spiritual needs and concerns. Amen.

BEATITUDES

Psalm 91

Daily Scripture

* Sunday:

A	B	C
Genesis 37:1-4, 12-28	2 Samuel 18:5-9, 15,	Isaiah 1:1, 10-20
Psalm 105:1-6,	31-33	Psalm 50:1-8, 22-23
16-22, 45*b*	Psalm 130	Hebrews 11:1-3,
Romans 10:5-15	Ephesians 4:25–5:2	8-16
Matthew 14:22-33	John 6:35, 41-51	Luke 12:32-40

* Monday:	Matthew 5:1-11
* Tuesday:	Genesis 12:1-3
* Wednesday:	Numbers 6:22-27
* Thursday:	Luke 1:39-45
* Friday:	Luke 6:20-23
* Saturday:	Romans 4:1-8

Meditation

To offer a beatitude is to bless a person. And Jesus begins his Sermon on the Mount with a list of blessings for his listeners. The catch is that many of us would willingly forgo the blessing if we did not have to undergo the condition Jesus is blessing.

Perhaps we need a different definition of blessing. Too often, our assumed definition of a "blessed life" is one in which we mostly get what we want. One of the most operative words in American public life these days is *rights*. And perhaps we have confused the idea of being blessed with obtaining our rights.

The source of each is different. To pursue what we have either as a political or personal right is to initiate action on our own behalf. Rights are earned or taken through a process of action for justice.

Blessings are bestowed by God directly or through the actions of other people. We can only be a recipient of blessings. We cannot pursue them. All we can do is open our hearts, minds, and hands to their possibility in our daily lives.

Perhaps our definition of what constitutes a blessing also needs to be expanded. Perhaps we need to ponder whether blessings are very simple gifts in our lives, rather than having all our needs met. Those who have lived long upon the earth know that a cold drink of water on a hot day, adequate food, and secure shelter can themselves be significant blessings.

In the Beatitudes, Jesus is talking of blessing as sustenance through suffering and final blessing for having endured pain and loss. And in these phrases, it is the state of existence that is being blessed. For if we do not mourn or be meek or hunger and thirst for righteousness, we will not be able to receive the comfort, inheritance, or fulfillment that is promised in the Beatitudes.

Until and unless we have lived in each of the spiritual places described in the Beatitudes, Jesus' teaching here remains a mystery. If you are in a state of sorrow, where is the consolation? But each of the states of existence Jesus blesses contains within it the motivation to find sustenance and endurance for living in it. The only alternative is just giving up, and giving up means giving up on the chance of being blessed.

One important way of making Scripture alive for us is to believe that such words as the Beatitudes are not time-limited. They are intended for each of us every day. On any day that we are living in one of the states listed in the Beatitudes, we can hear the promise of blessing Jesus would speak in our ears.

Guided Prayer

O God,

Today, I find myself living in the need of _____ as blessing from you. The area of my life that seems empty of blessing is _____

_____

_____.

I need the sustenance of _____

_____

_____.

I need solace because _____

_____

_____.

Soften my heart, O God, that I might receive the blessings I need. Lead me to someone who can be a conduit of your blessings in my life. In the name of one who knew both persecution and blessing. Amen.

THE GOOD SAMARITAN

Psalm 140

Daily Scripture

* Sunday:

A	B	C
Genesis 45:1-15	1 Kings 2:10-12, 3:3-14	Isaiah 5:1-7
Psalm 133	Psalm 111	Psalm 80:1-2, 8-19
Romans 11:1-2*a*,	Ephesians 5:15-20	Hebrews 11:29–12:2
29-32	John 6:51-58	Luke 12:49-56
Matthew 15:21-28		

* Monday:	Luke 10:25-37
* Tuesday:	Exodus 20:16-17
* Wednesday:	Leviticus 19:13-18
* Thursday:	Mark 12:28-34
* Friday:	Romans 13:8-10
* Saturday:	Matthew 18:15-20

Meditation

The story Jesus tells in response to the lawyer's question about neighbors is one of the most familiar biblical stories. The phrase "good Samaritan" has passed into secular language as one who helps out a stranger on the road. And initially, almost instinctively, Christians understand *the* meaning of the story to be compassion for the suffering stranger.

Of course, that is a primary meaning of the story when we are trying to determine whom we are to consider "neighbors." The phrase about the lawyer's motivation is a clue: "He wanted to vindicate himself." Usually we assume we can know whom we are to consider neighbors. But Jesus' definition is anyone in need; and given the racial hatred between Jews and Samaritans, *neighbor* includes those so different from us, we would rather not know them at all. For Jesus, *neighbor* includes our enemies and potentially all strangers.

I believe this story can function on another level as well, particularly for those Christians who are experiencing compassion fatigue from trying to walk a serious Christian walk as good Samaritans. One of the ways that this happens is to read through the story considering whether there is an area of our lives where we are the stranger, beaten and robbed on the road, rather than the Samaritan with all the resources.

Everyone is in need of a good Samaritan at some time in life, for we have all suffered involuntary loss. In those times, we need to consider what the symbols of the good Samaritan's explicit acts and help might mean for our own healing from hurt and loss.

Often a first step to healing is naming precisely what the hurt is. What part of our self has been beaten up? What has been robbed? And sometimes we wonder whether fellow Christians and ministers are going to walk by on the other side.

The good Samaritan offers a variety of kinds of solace to the man left along the side of the road. He is "moved with pity" and bathes and bandages wounds. He lifts him onto his own beast and walks himself. The Samaritan takes the man to an inn and looks after him as a close relative might and then pays the innkeeper for more care, promising reimbursement.

For yourself in compassion fatigue or burnout, what specifically might fill your needs for solace and comfort and healing like that which the Samaritan provided? Who are the persons who might be willing to offer that solace, and where is the inn where you might rest from your labors?

To attend to our own needs by following through on the answers to these questions is to learn the skill of self-nurture. Self-nurture is a fairly strange concept for Christians because we believe that we are to concentrate on others' needs. But spiritual and emotional self-nurture is required in order to find restoration for our bodies and souls so that we can once again offer wholehearted compassion to our neighbors.

Guided Prayer

Dear God,

I know how to be a good Samaritan. The church has taught me well. But I don't like to consider when I might be in the ditch. What if no one but priests and Levites comes by?

My spiritual wound that needs compassionate attention is _____

_____

_____.

Lead me to the healing that I need.

How do I learn to nurture my spirit and my faith and my tired discipleship? Show me your way, O God. Lead me in your truth for me. Amen.

BEING LOST, BECOMING FOUND

Psalm 139

Daily Scripture

* Sunday:

A	B	C
Exodus 1:8–2:10	1 Kings 8:22-30, 41-43	Jeremiah 1:4-10
Psalm 124	Psalm 84	Psalm 71:1-6
Romans 12:1-8	Ephesians 6:10-20	Hebrews 12:18-29
Matthew 16:13-20	John 6:56-69	Luke 13:10-17

* Monday:	Matthew 18:10-14
* Tuesday:	Luke 15:3-7
* Wednesday:	Luke 15:8-10
* Thursday:	Luke 15:11-32
* Friday:	Luke 19:1-10
* Saturday:	Philippians 3:7-11

Meditation

Few children escape the experience of being momentarily lost from parents or family. As adults, we may not remember the looming size of unfamiliar streets, buildings, and space.

Once, visiting a distant cousin's store in an unfamiliar Illinois town, I walked out the wrong door alone. I found myself on a street I had never seen before. Disoriented, I walked a short distance before realizing I was lost. Part of the panic was realizing that I didn't know whether my family knew that I was lost and whether they would even be looking for me. If they didn't look for me, how could I be found?

Jesus' parables about the lost sheep and lost coin describe God as a devoted seeker of those who are lost. The shepherd is delighted to find one sheep lost out of a hundred. Thus each of us is precious to God. And the response is rejoicing by all friends and neighbors who are brought together by the good news.

Jesus' parable about the lost coin and the woman's search for it brings a poignant image of our sense of being lost from God. What crack have we rolled into? What hides us from the search of One who considers us so valuable that everyone would be told and finding us would be a cause for community celebration?

The context of these two parables is public accusation of Jesus who, as a friend to sinners, sits at table with them. The parables are told as revelation of the importance of lost sinners in relation to those righteous ones doing the accusing.

It is very easy to get lost. We can be lost from ourselves. We can be lost from the everyday moorings of our life when crisis happens. We can feel lost from friends and family when there is alienation or misunderstanding.

These parables are told in the context of Jesus' definition of sin as being lost from God. And the motion in God's search for us when we are lost from God in some unconfessed sin is that when we turn in repentance, then God and all the angels rejoice.

This is a very different picture from the one most of us have of sin and confession. Our Christian tradition seems to convey that repentance is a mode of trauma and shame. But in these parables, the implication is that the state of unconfessed sin is like the panic and fear we experience when we are physically lost.

And the response of God is not judgment on our sin but rejoicing at our repentance. In these parables, after repentance there is a party.

Guided Prayer

Dear God,

I have a difficult time understanding that I am so precious to you that others would be left behind while you search for me. I do understand what it is to be lost.

Right now I feel lost from _____

_____

_____.

I need reassurance that you are seeking me whenever and wherever I am lost.

The sin I would confess this day is _____

_____

_____.

I want to learn to trust that angels rejoice each time I confess my sins to you. In the name of Jesus, the Good Shepherd, Amen.

ABIDING IN JESUS

Psalm 72

Daily Scripture

* Sunday:

A	B	C
Exodus 3:1-15	Song of Solomon 2:8-13	Jeremiah 2:4-13
Psalm 105:1-6, 23-26, 45c	Psalm 45:1-2, 6-9 James 1:17-27	Psalm 81:1, 10-16 Hebrews 13:1-8,
Romans 12:9-21	Mark 7:1-8, 14-15,	15-16
Matthew 16:21-28	21-23	Luke 14:1, 7-14

* Monday:	John 15:1-11
* Tuesday:	John 15:12-17
* Wednesday:	1 John 2:23-28
* Thursday:	1 John 4:7-16
* Friday:	Romans 8:1-11
* Saturday:	2 Corinthians 5:16-20

Meditation

Jesus lived and ministered mostly among folks who lived close to the land. Thus his parables and stories often used agricultural metaphors that would be immediately relevant to his listeners.

One startling idea in the John 15 passage is the notion that Jesus himself needed pruning. There should be reassurance for all of us in the idea that Jesus' humanity also required pruning of those elements in him that were not fruitful.

The important word here is that old-fashioned one, *abide.* We are to abide in Jesus just as the spirit of Jesus abides in us due to salvation. We are to rest in Jesus, to wait in Jesus, and to live in Jesus. By this abiding we ourselves become more spiritually fruitful and thus have more to offer to needy persons who seek something more in their lives but often cannot express their need for communion with God.

The level of spiritual dependence on Jesus implied by the image of the vine and branches can be threatening to us if being in control is a major personal impetus. For abiding in Jesus means leaning on those "everlasting arms" for our deepest needs.

In the church that has nurtured my adult faith, there is a mahogany cross hung in the baptistry. As a Celtic cross pointing to the wholeness of God and the gospel, there is a beaten brass circle just behind the intersection of the cross. Baptistry lights that shine on the cross create a shadow effect that is reassuring every time I look at that cross.

For the image of the shadow is one of an abstract head above rounded shoulders and arms curved out to anyone who chooses to look and see them. In this shadow, created by lights shining on the cross of pain and humiliation, there is a place of abiding; and that place of abiding is centered in the arms of Jesus.

When we lean there, when we abide there, we are close to the heart of Jesus on the cross. We are close to both the pain of that reality and the love that reaches out to us beyond the cross. Both pain and love come together when our hearts abide in Jesus.

When we abide there, then we too are filled with the love of the Spirit. We are attached, like branches to a vine, to the love, joy, mercy, and grace of God.

Guided Prayer

Dear God,

Abiding in Jesus sounds like a comforting image. But I know that is not all there is to the teaching. What about my faith and Christian witness needs pruning?

I would bear the fruit of _____

_____

_____

to _____

_____

_____.

I want to abide in your love. Set my heart free from trivial concerns that I might better learn to follow your commandments. In the name of Jesus, the true Vine, Amen.

SEEKING TRUTH

Psalm 51

Daily Scripture

* Sunday:

A	B	C
Exodus 12:1-14	Proverbs 22:1-2,	Jeremiah 18:1-11
Psalm 149	8-9, 22-23	Psalm 139:1-6, 13-18
Romans 13:8-14	Psalm 125	Philemon 1-21
Matthew 18:15-20	James 2:1-10, 14-17	Luke 14:25-33
	Mark 7:24-37	

* Monday:	Isaiah 59:9-20
* Tuesday:	Jeremiah 5:1-3
* Wednesday:	Zechariah 8:11-17
* Thursday:	John 4:7-26
* Friday:	John 8:31-47
* Saturday:	1 Peter 1:17-25

Meditation

Recently the local paper has reviewed books and expert opinions on Americans' increasing comfort with lies, both personal and public. Statistics indicate that most people admit to lying and expect lying to be a part of everyday life, even smoothing over the rough spots caused by literal truth-telling. The connotation of the comments seems to be that truth-telling is harsh and uncomfortable, that truth "hurts" and that lying makes human interaction easier.

Curiously enough, the teaching of Jesus has a focus different from what we usually think in regard to ethics in truth-telling. Jesus repeatedly taught that we are to *seek* the truth and that his gospel of redemption was the truth of God. The phrase in John 8 that we shall know the truth and the truth shall make us free is a promise that eludes many of us.

One interpretation of this teaching is that it is only when we know all of the truth about ourselves that we can be truly free. Such truth-seeking about our own whole personhood is a life-long endeavor. And what that search brings is freedom from self-delusion, the lies we tell ourselves about ourselves in order to make our own daily way more smooth.

The doctrine of original sin and its corollary of total depravity of the human soul certainly make the search for personal truth in light of Jesus' teaching less appealing. If we believe that the basic truth about ourselves is mostly or absolutely sinful, we certainly aren't going to volunteer for the self-despising which that belief incurs.

The notion that we all actually have original blessing by virtue of our creation in the image of God might make a search for the whole truth about ourselves more appealing. A focus on the truth of our original blessing means that we can find out more about our capacities for goodness, for love and compassion, and for growth toward the truth that makes us free.

Of course, the whole, complex truth about our humanity is that we are both filled with a propensity to sin and also that we have been originally blessed by God's determination that we should exist in the world. Searching for our own whole truth means moving into and through the sins of self-delusion and denial.

And finding the truth of God about our own creation means shouldering the responsibility of living out our days as persons who are blessed by God. In doing that we become capable of blessing others by bearing the image of Jesus Christ in the world.

Guided Prayer

Dear God,

    We live in a world in which it is hard to tell the truth. People don't want to hear the truth.

    What truth do I need to learn about myself as a person and as a Christian? Teach me the truth that will make me more free of self-delusion.

    I need to experience the original blessing of _____

_____

_____.

    I will seek your face, O God, so that I may know your blessing and grow into the responsibility of bearing the image of Christ. In the name of Jesus, Amen.

JUDGMENT

Psalm 7

Daily Scripture

* Sunday:

A	B	C
Exodus 14:19-31	Proverbs 1:20-33	Jeremiah 4:11-12, 22-28
Psalm 114	Psalm 19	Psalm 14
Romans 14:1-12	James 3:1-12	1 Timothy 1:12-17
Matthew 18:21-35	Mark 8:27-38	Luke 15:1-10

* Monday:	Matthew 7:1-5
* Tuesday:	Luke 7:37-48
* Wednesday:	John 8:3-11
* Thursday:	Romans 2:1-11
* Friday:	1 Corinthians 4:1-5
* Saturday:	James 4:11-12

Meditation

We do it all the time; we make judgments continually in order to make the necessary decisions of our lives. So where is the line when judging others becomes wrong for a Christian?

Perhaps what Jesus was trying to teach is the difference between human standards and God's standards. For we tend to operate in the same mode of human judgment about one another as Christians as we do when making decisions about what job to take or what contractor to hire or whom to date. In those human decisions we evaluate competency or appeal or value.

The judgment that Jesus refers to has to do with moral and spiritual evaluation of the worth of another person's attitude, words, or behavior. And the message is that first we are to do an examination of what might be clouding our own view.

This is one of the hardest teachings of Jesus to practice. Judging one another's reasons or motivations seems just to come naturally to us. But the first consideration is to consider what our own motivation might be in a given situation. This calls for time out for reflection and for honesty with ourselves. It certainly is a lot easier to just pass judgment.

Just as none of us can know all of God, neither can we ever know all of the aims, needs, and desires of another human being, even if we have lived with that person for decades. The Bible teaches that God looks on the heart of every human being and God's judgment of us comes out of that.

So, after we have looked inward at our own motivation when we are tempted to judge another, the next fruit of the Spirit we need to pray for is patience. There are nearly always personal reasons why people behave as they do, and when we are mystified or hurt or angry, we need patience to hear them out about what those might be.

Not judging others is an act of humility. Resisting the temptation to judge means we are admitting that we don't always know best in every situation. Resisting our willingness to judge others is also following the Golden Rule. For, generally, we would prefer not to have our own motivations put under the microscope of someone else's judgment. And according to the gospel, that is exactly what will happen to us when we judge others.

Guided Prayer

Dear God,

I don't know what your judgment of me might be. And most days I am afraid to ask because I know that I fall short.

I am most sorely tempted to judge _____

about _____

_____

_____.

I am anxious that _____

go well, and so I carry the judgment that _____

might _____

_____

_____.

What is the mote in my own eye? What motivation of mine

about _____

do I need to consider first?

Grant the increase of humility and patience in my considerations of and relationships with others. In Jesus' name, Amen.

PERSISTENCE IN PRAYER

Psalm 28

Daily Scripture

* Sunday:

A	B	C
Exodus 16:2-15	Proverbs 31:10-31	Jeremiah 8:18–9:1
Psalm 105:1-6, 37-45	Psalm 1	Psalm 79:1-9
Philippians 1:21-30	James 3:13–4:3, 7-8a	1 Timothy 2:1-7
Matthew 20:1-16	Mark 9:30-37	Luke 16:1-13

* Monday:	Luke 18:1-8
* Tuesday:	1 Samuel 1:3-17
* Wednesday:	Psalm 4
* Thursday:	Psalm 5
* Friday:	Isaiah 56:1-8
* Saturday:	Philippians 4:4-7

Meditation

One of my personal maxims is that stubbornness is really a virtue. Sometimes the only difference between success and failure is the refusal to give up. We have only to consider the history of human progress against disease to realize that it is the persistence of scientists and doctors that has wrought healing in many lives.

Perhaps our theology is at fault when we function in prayer as if once we have mentioned a petition, then God has heard it and we don't need to do anything else. But there are multiple examples in Scripture of vehement prayer, which model persistence for us.

Moses both interceded with God for the Israelites and begged God to take them off his hands. He was constantly in touch with Yahweh during that forty-year trek through the desert.

Isaiah contended with God; Jeremiah pleaded for judgment; Hannah prayed so fervently that the priest thought she was drunk.

In Jesus' story of the persistent widow, we are told of a woman who simply will not give up on her petition for justice with an unfair judge. It is her persistence alone that overcomes the judge's intention to ignore her since she obviously has no social, political, or economic power to leverage his response.

Why does Jesus use such a harsh example as the model for our prayers to God? There seems to be a message that we can contend with God for justice on our own behalf and that persistence in prayer is important.

During a period of time when both my former husband and I lost our jobs and there were a number of other family crises, I learned to contend with God. Living in a state of reacting to crisis as best we could and seldom getting beyond survival mode lasted for several years.

I came to believe only in a providence of survival; I could not believe there was a providence of flourishing and joy for us. I railed at God that we had had more than our share of trauma and that we had done the best we knew to do and we still seemed to make little progress toward security. And life lived in survival mode was unfair to two sons who simply had to deal with the fact that their parents were assaulted by trends and decisions beyond their control. So I contended with God on behalf of my whole family.

Prayer became both more honest and more constant during this period. At times, God really did feel to me like an unjust judge. At times, I wasn't certain that my heart-rending petitions were getting a hearing.

But I persisted. And months later, I came to believe that flourishing and justice were possible.

Guided Prayer

Dear God,

I would contend with you, O God, about _____

_____

_____.

The justice I seek and need manifest in my life is _____

_____

_____.

I will cry to you day and night for _____

_____

_____.

Hear me, O Lord. Give ear to my petition. Bring justice quickly for the sake of all of us who need your strong providence. Amen.

A BROKEN SPIRIT

Psalm 51

Daily Scripture

* Sunday:

A	B	C
Exodus 17:1-7	Esther 7:1-6, 9-10,	Jeremiah 32:1-3,
Psalm 78:1-4, 12-16	9:20-22	6-15
Philippians 2:1-13	Psalm 124	Psalm 91:1-6, 14-16
Matthew 21:23-32	James 5:13-20	1 Timothy 6:6-19
	Mark 9:38-50	Luke 16:19-31

* Monday:	Job 16:6–17:1
* Tuesday:	Psalm 31
* Wednesday:	Psalm 119:1-11
* Thursday:	Psalm 119:26-32
* Friday:	Psalm 119:169-176
* Saturday:	1 John 5:1-5

Meditation

To be honest, I have never even liked the idea of submission. As a woman battling enforced submission in a reactionary denomination, there was little room for considering exactly what submission meant to me in prayer and spiritual formation.

Teaching about submission implies that, like salvation, it is a one-time decision. The teaching I heard implied some experience that would lead me to once and for all find the will of God and submit to it. In conversation with a friend, I acknowledged that relinquishment of certain aspects of my life and personal myths that kept me from being who God made me to be was as close as I could get to what submission seemed to mean. But submission as a life mode seemed impossible.

Another reservation is that I believe that submission is highly individualized. That is, the teaching was always so vague and generalized that I thought both the process and the end were the same for everyone. My issues for submission are not the same as my sister's or brother's.

The promise in Psalm 51 that God does not despise the sacrifice of a broken spirit has become the opening for me about the subject of submission. One day in agonized prayer over the church's theological oppression of women, I cried out to God in great emotional and spiritual pain. And the words that came were, "This is how we are broken."

This does not mean that God brings pain into our lives in order to bring us to submission. That is not who the loving God of Scripture and Jesus is.

But the broken spirit is a form of sacrifice. Sacrifice is not self-denial. The word refers in Scripture to what is offered up to God so that God might deem the offering sacred. We don't get to decide whether our offering is worthy. And submission of our offering, of the parts of our selves, even of our pain, is an acknowledgment of God's power and authority to intervene in our lives.

To submit, to be in submission to God, is to be in the posture of offering up as much of ourselves as we can at whatever place on the spiritual journey we find ourselves. To be in the posture of submission is to acknowledge that all of who we are and all of what we possess are gifts from God. We have not created ourselves or our talents.

For persons raised in American culture that prizes individualism, self-sufficiency, and achievement, submission is probably the hardest spiritual discipline to accept and learn to practice. We are disciples; we follow a Teacher who submitted to the mission of God for his life. We can learn lessons for our lives by offering up in prayer the burdens, traumas, and proud strengths of our selves.

Guided Prayer

Dear God,

There are so many obligations in my life. Much of what I submit to are results of previous decisions I don't feel able to reconsider. The heaviest one right now is _____

_____

_____.

So I come with a beleaguered spirit to ask, What relinquishment is needed in my spiritual life on this day?

Perhaps it is simply my sense of self-sufficiency about _____

_____

_____.

There are days I do not know whether I can give up anything else. On those days, revive my joy and strengthen my spirit. Amen.

HARVEST OF RIGHTEOUSNESS

Psalm 112

Daily Scripture

* Sunday:

A	B	C
Exodus 20:1-4, 7-9, 12-20	Job 1:1, 2:1-10	Lamentations 1:1-6, 3:19-26
Psalm 19	Psalm 26	Psalm 37:1-9
Philippians 3:4*b*-14	Hebrews 1:1-4, 2:5-12	2 Timothy 1:1-14
Matthew 21:33-46	Mark 10:2-16	Luke 17:5-10

* Monday: Isaiah 32:14-18
* Tuesday: Isaiah 61
* Wednesday: Jeremiah 22:1-5
* Thursday: Matthew 5:13-20
* Friday: Romans 3:19-26
* Saturday: 2 Corinthians 9:6-15

Meditation

My family will never let me forget the chilly October day that I stood, ankle deep in mud, determined to get enough you-pick-it broccoli to see us through the winter. Each autumn for a number of years I seemed to function under the instinct that compelled me to make certain there was ample strawberry jam, applesauce, broccoli, and corn stored up for the cold weather.

In the Second Corinthians reading Paul indicates that sowing and reaping are aspects of the spiritual life as well. The primary meaning in this passage does not mean that we can sow righteousness in order to reap it, though that is a common misperception of the images. Instead, Paul is declaring a form of natural consequences for growth in faith and spiritual life. We cannot sow in order to reap, but the degree of our investment of time and energy in spiritual life will determine the kind and degree of harvest we are likely to have.

Psalm 112 reveals the impact of a life sown in righteousness. Such spiritual "seed" is sown generously and broadly. The righteousness of such a person endures forever. It does not end with physical death, but lives on in the lives of those persons whom the righteous person has ministered to.

Righteousness is a touchy word for Christians. There is a very fine line between the righteousness that is taught and encouraged in such passages and the self-righteousness that is exemplified by the Pharisees and criticized by Jesus. The key to a distinction is the biblical notion that God looks on the heart. God knows whether our true motivation for following the commandments and seeking spiritual depth in prayer and service is a matter of an open, contrite heart.

The righteousness that lasts is lived out of the fervent, honest seeking of God's purpose in our lives. The righteousness that is a response to human expectations or with the expectation of human awareness is short-lived.

The actual determination of the harvest of Christian righteousness is a matter of the movement of the Holy Spirit. We are not capable of knowing or deciding what impact our righteousness might have; that is God's initiative. What we have are the seeds of righteousness given to us as spiritual gifts by God in Christ. We cast those seeds and gifts abroad in the world and leave the increase up to God.

In our lifetime, we will see and know some of the harvest of our righteousness, of a sincere heart's search for God's leading in prayer and a life lived in service. Some of it we will never know about. But other people will know, and the work of Christ's kingdom on earth will benefit.

Guided Prayer

Dear God,

Righteousness is a heavy word. I try to be a good person and know there are days in which I fail miserably. Right now the hardest place for me to be a Christian example is _____

_____

_____.

The person who challenges my impulse toward the good more than any other is _____

_____

_____.

Convict me about the persons and places where I need to sow the seeds of righteousness. What would you have me do?

May I learn to give and help without thought of return. In Jesus' name, Amen.

GATHERING IN

Psalm 138

Daily Scripture

* Sunday:

A	B	C
Exodus 32:1-14	Job 23:1-9, 16-17	Jeremiah 29:1, 4-7
Psalm 106:1-6, 19-23	Psalm 22:1-15	Psalm 66:1-12
Philippians 4:1-9	Hebrews 4:12-16	2 Timothy 2:8-15
Matthew 22:1-14	Mark 10:17-31	Luke 17:11-19

* Monday:	Deuteronomy 28:1-9
* Tuesday:	Proverbs 8:1-3, 27-36
* Wednesday:	Isaiah 44:1-8
* Thursday:	Ezekiel 34:25-31
* Friday:	John 16:20-24
* Saturday:	Philippians 4:4-13

Meditation

One of the effects of our fast-paced lifestyles is that we often do not make time to dwell on our blessings. An old gospel hymn instructs us to "Count your blessings, name them one by one. Count your many blessings, see what God has done." When we stay too busy to count our blessings, the difficulties and problems of our lives can become overwhelming.

Another result of a hectic lifestyle is that many Christians walk around without an experiential definition of beneficence. We do not relish the good things that happen long enough or deeply enough to develop a secure sense of the beneficence in our lives.

Once during a very painful time in my life, I developed the image of letting every good thing that happened, every word of affirmation and encouragement fall deeply inside. I imagined all those words and acts of compassion which came from family, friends, and church as filling up something that had lived empty inside me for a long time. I was filling up that empty space with good things, with the beneficence that life offered me.

This is another arena where our American individualism tends to cut us off from the beneficent care that everyone needs at one time or another. One cold February I was sick with the flu, and like most mothers with busy families, I was on my own to do what I needed to get well. But a friend called, heard the misery in my voice, and made two trips to offer beneficence. First she brought a pot of soup, and then she came back with spring flowers to cheer my spirits. Such intentional, proactive caring brought me the live experience of beneficence in my life, and her acts are still on my list of life blessings.

Beneficence is different from compassion. Compassion is feeling and intent. Beneficence is doing. Beneficence is proactive and takes initiative to offer hospitable space and "random acts of kindness."

We all need beneficence at one time or another. The pace of our lives almost makes giving and receiving acts of beneficence a luxury. Each of us will have those times when we aren't receiving what we need. At those times we need to count our blessings.

Graduation from seminary at age 44 gave me permission to throw my own party in celebration. What I never expected was graduation presents. After all the guests left, I sat on the couch with the unexpected gifts in my lap. I gathered them in with a sense of astonishment at the beneficence proffered by my friends.

Whatever our life experience, we have a harvest of blessings. We can gather in beneficence and let kindness that has come to us fall deep within and fill us with gratitude for the providence of God.

Guided Prayer

Dear God,

Thank you for the beneficence of _____

_____

_____

in my life right now. The great blessings I am grateful for are _____

_____

and _____

and _____

You are a mighty and glorious God who has poured blessings of

_____

_____

into my life.

Make my heart supple that I may notice the overflowing cup of blessings in my life. Teach me to count my blessings every day. Amen.

FALLOWNESS

Psalm 130

Daily Scripture

* Sunday:

A	B	C
Exodus 33:12-23	Job 38:1-7	Jeremiah 31:27-34
Psalm 99	Psalm 104:1-9, 24,	Psalm 119:97-104
1 Thessalonians 1:1-10	35c	2 Timothy 3:14–4:5
Matthew 22:15-22	Hebrews 5:1-10	Luke 18:1-8
	Mark 10:35-45	

* Monday:	Isaiah 30:18-21
* Tuesday:	Isaiah 40:28-31
* Wednesday:	Lamentations 3:22-28
* Thursday:	Psalm 25
* Friday:	Luke 10:38-42
* Saturday:	2 Peter 3:11-15a

Meditation

Afriend traveling in the Midwest described the rich, dark earth undulating in plowed furrows as far as she could see. The land at that point was fallow, awaiting seed or perhaps resting. One piece of wisdom from experienced farmers and gardeners is that certain fields and beds need to lie fallow on a regular basis. The land that feeds us needs to rest.

In the cycle of seasons, winter is the time in which the earth and plants that grow in it are fallow. They rest, storing nutrients and waiting through the cold for the gradual change in the earth's axis which turns our hemisphere toward the sun and begins the burgeoning of green growth once more.

The wisdom of fallowness is one that is unfamiliar to busy, achievement-oriented Americans. We tend to think we are always supposed to *do* something. Perhaps we need to pay closer attention to the fallowness of the earth and learn how the state of fallowness might enhance our prayer life and faith.

To be fallow is to be in a state of rest, ready for what comes next, but not yet productive. One of the lessons of middle age is the body's need for simple rest in addition to sleep. Personally, I've learned to appreciate the art and benefits of snoozing.

My spiritual journey has always had the intentional motion of searching for God. But one day in Old Testament class, my professor read a passage from the book of Proverbs about the Wisdom of God searching for us. That was both a challenging and comforting epiphany for my busyholic lifestyle. I wasn't totally responsible for my relationship with God. I could actually let go and let God in Wisdom search for me and find me in whatever state I was in. Further reflection on this image of being sought by Wisdom brought the realization that what I had been seeking was varieties of wisdom about God and faith, the church and human relationships.

The message from Proverbs was that all along Wisdom had likewise been searching for me. In fact, both my seeking and Wisdom's seeking of me were inexplicably one and the same journey. We had been traveling together; I just didn't know the Wisdom of God was a life companion before that day in class.

To be fallow in our daily schedules is to stop outrunning God. To be fallow in our hearts is to learn the peace of waiting upon the Lord. To be fallow in our spirits is to live and pray in a spirit of readiness for what growth might be needed in the next season of life and faith.

Guided Prayer

Dear God,

Like Martha, I have been worried and distracted by too many things. My heart needs rest because _____

_____

_____.

My spirit needs rest because _____

_____

_____.

But I am afraid if I stop to be fallow, that _____

_____

_____

might _____

_____

_____.

Bring your Wisdom close to me that I might learn to be fallow and know the peace which passes all understanding. In the name of Jesus who went apart to pray, Amen.

HEART WINTER

Psalm 31

Daily Scripture

* Sunday:

A	B	C
Deuteronomy 34:1-12	Job 42:1-6, 10-17	Joel 2:23-32
Psalm 90:1-6, 13-17	Psalm 34:1-8	Psalm 65
1 Thessalonians 2:1-8	Hebrews 7:23-28	2 Timothy 4:6-8, 16-18
Matthew 22:34-46	Mark 10:46-52	Luke 18:9-14

* Monday:	Job 30:15-28
* Tuesday:	Lamentations 3:1-18
* Wednesday:	Micah 7:1-10
* Thursday:	Psalm 18:1-30
* Friday:	John 1:1-14
* Saturday:	1 Thessalonians 5:1-11

Meditation

One autumn an acute dread of winter came to me. As the days shortened, I mourned the loss of daylight each day. The early dusk came to stand for the fact that winter would mean less light every day for a number of months. A winter of the heart had set in.

In the deep of winter on retreat, I woke early and waited what seemed like forever for the dawn light to come. Since there was a dense cloud cover, I could see snow beneath the trees and the sky did eventually go from black to blue-gray. But dawn, the warm colors of the sun rising, did not come.

Perhaps I was in touch with the primitive in myself which feared that even though light would come, it would not be warm light. And if no warm light came, how would winter ever end?

This is what the winter of the heart is. Whether it is emotional depression, despair, or a spiritual dark night, what paralyzes us is the fear that the blue-gray light of pain and loss and the iced-over pond of our heart will not know true sunlight and warmth again. It is not the loss of all light in our lives. We can usually find something to call good in our lives. But a winter of the heart means that we do not know the warm light of faith and hope. There is no warmth to promise spring and new growth in our souls and lives.

Living in the winter of the heart or spirit, we find enough light to go on; but it is still cold light. It is light that lets us see but does not warm our hearts or encourage our spirits.

The Gospel of John promises that darkness will not overcome us. That is because Jesus as the Light of the world is still available to be present as Christ to us in prayer, Scripture, worship, and Communion.

Sometimes living in the winter of the heart, it is almost impossible to believe that. We may scoff at either being able to experience the presence of Christ in our lives, or we may doubt the power of Christ to work in us to bring the warmth of faith and hope once more. Sometimes the hardest part is just making the first move to renew any spiritual discipline that has fed and encouraged us in the past.

But we can pray the dread. We can pray our fears and even our disbelief. The worst thing we can do while trying to live in a winter of the heart is hide that from God and try to solve it on our own. Sometimes it does take the human effort of getting therapy or spiritual counsel from responsible persons. But there are lessons of faith to be learned even from a winter of the heart. And God in Jesus Christ is our teacher.

Guided Prayer

Dear God,

The shortened days and cold air are enough to deal with when winter comes, O God. When my heart is heavy, I fear _____

_____

_____.

The dread in my life this year is about _____

_____

_____.

Sometimes doubt just descends, O God. And more than anything else at those times, I need _____

_____

_____.

To believe that the darkness is not dark to you, as the psalmist says, is difficult to understand. Your mystery is beyond my comprehension.

Bring the warm comfort of your presence near. Lead me to the ways, the spiritual habits that will encourage my faith. Amen.

SOLITUDE

Psalm 62

Daily Scripture

* Sunday:

A	B	C
Joshua 3:7-17	Ruth 1:1-18	Habukkuk 1:1-4, 2:1-4
Psalm 107:1-7, 33-37	Psalm 146	Psalm 119:137-144
1 Thessalonians 2:9-13, 17-20	Hebrews 9:11-14	2 Thessalonians 1:1-4, 11-12
Matthew 23:1-12	Mark 12:28-34	Luke 19:1-10

* Monday:	Genesis 16:1-15
* Tuesday:	Genesis 32:22-31
* Wednesday:	Jeremiah 15:16-21
* Thursday:	Matthew 4:1-11
* Friday:	Mark 6:30-32, 45-47
* Saturday:	John 16:25-33

Meditation

The quick and easy distinction between loneliness and solitude is that solitude is sought and chosen, and loneliness is not. Loneliness is a painful experience for anyone no matter age or station in life. To feel lonely is to feel unwanted, to be without companionship or understanding. Thus it is possible to feel lonely in the middle of a crowd of people. It is even possible to feel lonely surrounded by family and friends.

Most people have personality characteristics that lean toward either the extrovert or introvert end of the spectrum. Loneliness can be painful for extroverts because other people are a main source of joy their in life. Solitude can be threatening because it might remind an extrovert of feeling lonely. Introverts tend to enjoy their own company and seek solitude for recuperation from the stresses of life, but they can get stuck in isolation.

Solitude is considered a leading spiritual discipline and becomes ever more significant as our lives and schedules become more complex and hectic. Solitude as a spiritual discipline is withdrawal from the things of the world in order to be open to communion with God alone.

Sometimes God gets our attention by dramatic events in our personal, even public lives. But much more often, God's "voice" is the "still, small voice" discerned only when we follow Jesus' example and withdraw to a quiet place for a time of intentional listening to the leading of God. If we depend on the times of God's clear breaking-in to our lives, we risk living many days without a vibrant sense of the presence of God.

Solitary, personal retreats have become the most immediate means of intentionally seeking the presence of God for many persons. What such retreats do is signal to our hearts and minds that we are explicitly setting aside time for the development of our relationship with God. Solitude for the purpose of prayer and meditation is weaving and setting out the welcome mat for God.

One of the important lessons of solitude is increasing confidence in our ability to lean on God for the gifts of the spirit which comfort and enhance our faith and spiritual equilibrium. Early on in my retreats, I kept the schedule of a busyholic. I collected a stack of books from the library, took some handwork, and kept a journal and pen with me at all times. In that way, I was maintaining control over what would happen on the retreat and seldom encountered the Comforter.

To be truly in solitude before God is to follow the Scripture's dictum to wait on the Lord. The immediate insecure question is, What if God doesn't show up? But in solitude we learn that God is always seeking us and that solitude itself is one way to say yes to God's seeking. It is also making prayer a priority and taking the posture of a humble student willing to be taught by God whatever it is that God deems we need to know.

By going to solitude, we create a hospitable place in our hearts and lives for the presence of God.

Guided Prayer

Dear God,

   I find sometimes that I am afraid of solitude. I am afraid of feeling lonely or of being bored. What if I go away to a quiet place seeking you and do not feel your presence?
   I need solitude in order to _____

_____

_____.

   If I make solitude a goal, I would hope to find _____

_____

_____

in that space.

   I want to say yes to your seeking me. I want to know communion with you and to learn how to live and move and have my being in your abiding peace. Amen.

SILENCE

Psalm 62

Daily Scripture

* **Sunday:**

A	B	C
Joshua 24:1-3*a*, 14-25	Ruth 3:1-5, 4:13-17	Haggai 1:15*b*–2:9
Psalm 78:1-7	Psalm 127	Psalm 145:1-5, 17-21
1 Thessalonians 4:13-18	Hebrews 9:24-28	2 Thessalonians 2:1-5, 13-17
Matthew 25:1-13	Mark 12:38-44	Luke 20:27-38

* **Monday:**	Ecclesiastes 5:1-6
* **Tuesday:**	Isaiah 30:15, 18
* **Wednesday:**	Psalm 81:6-16
* **Thursday:**	Psalm 131
* **Friday:**	Proverbs 11:12-13
* **Saturday:**	1 Thessalonians 4:9-12

Meditation

We live in a very noisy world. Amid traffic outside and computer beeps at work and television at home, most of us experience true silence only occasionally. Sometimes we are afraid of silence; we do not want issues and agendas we usually avoid to surface in our minds and hearts. Sometimes we avoid silence because we do not want to hear the voice of God.

The mystics tell us that silence is essential to formation of the spiritual life. Silence is essential to the hearing of that still, small voice which we spend most of our waking hours ignoring.

Silence and solitude tend to go together in the heart of the person who intends to listen to the movement of the Holy Spirit. Even the frustration at not getting enough silence can be a gift because such frustration leads us to go away to a quiet place to seek the presence of God once more.

Jesus gave us a clear example of leaving the crowds and noise and commerce behind in order to find silent communion with God. And a quiet place allows us to let our heart, mind, and spirit find the calm that is a prerequisite to deep prayer, opened to the movement of the Spirit in our lives. Silence is necessary in order to be open to possibility, to what new thing God might be doing in our lives.

The back lake at Loretto is usually deserted. In all my retreats I have seldom encountered another person there. And because there is animal life, silence is not absolute. But usually I realize that what I seek is not absolute silence, but the silence of nature which is a palpable silence broken occasionally by the whistling tweet of a meadowlark or croak of a frog.

So it is in nature, far from the sounds of human creation, that I find the outer silence which nurtures inner silence. God does not impose the presence of the Spirit on our lives. The presence of the Spirit of God must be invited and welcomed. And we have to go away from the distractions of our daily life and the noises of human creation in order to be able to extend the invitation with enough space and time to be quiet and listen.

Regular retreats as a spiritual discipline help form the habit of silence as a spiritual discipline. I began to find in going to Loretto that my soul would become quiet and calm as the car approached the turn. The palpable silence of God's creation in nature always came to heal the invasions of human noise. And when I turned to God in silence, God always had a message for me.

Guided Prayer

Dear God,

When I think of silencing all the daily noise and words, I find I am afraid of _____

_____

_____.

My busy, noisy life keeps me from acknowledging _____

_____

_____.

Where can I go to find silence? Where is the place that will calm my heart?

Lead me to silence, O God. Make me to search for those times and places where I will know the repose of my soul in your gracious presence. Amen.

LOVE OF GOD

Psalm 143

Daily Scripture

*Sunday:

A	B	C
Judges 4:1-7	1 Samuel 1:4-20	Isaiah 65:17-25, 12
Psalm 123	2:1-10	Psalm 98
1 Thessalonians 5:1-11	Psalm 16	1 Thessalonians 3:6-13
Matthew 25:14-30	Hebrews 10:11-14,	Luke 21:5-19
	19-25	
	Mark 13:1-8	

*Monday:	Deuteronomy 7:7-13
*Tuesday:	Isaiah 54:4-10
*Wednesday:	Jeremiah 31:1-14
*Thursday:	Hosea 11:1-8
*Friday:	1 Corinthians 13:1-13
*Saturday:	1 John 4:7-19

Meditation

One of the recurring phrases in the Psalms is "steadfast love." Referring to the steadfast love of God, the psalmist sometimes praises God for this love, sometimes pleads for a sign of love, and sometimes vows belief in God's love.

One of the most difficult spiritual lessons is learning in faith that the love of God is sufficient for our needs as individual persons. Perhaps those persons we consider saints in everyday life around us are those Christians who have learned that God's love is sufficient and who have learned to trust in that assurance.

Perhaps we have difficulty learning the lesson of the love of God because we do not know how to find or experience the reality of God's love in our lives. Perhaps we label as luck or fortune or our own achievement what is actually the functioning of God's beneficent love in our lives. A rooted belief in God's intention to love and care for us in all ways can change our attitudes and interpretation of the events of our lives.

One warm, sunny July day I discovered an image of God's steadfast love in our lives. Gone for a meandering wade in the New River in North Carolina, I headed for a jutting rock to just sit and watch the sunlight on water and listen to the gurgle of the river over rocks. Sitting there pondering a tiny waterfall in the constant flow of the river, I stuck my hand in to feel the current. At that moment, the rapidly flowing water became a symbol of God's steadfast love. At any given spot in a river, there is no way to know where the moving water comes from or goes. We are not in control of the stream; the river flows on. The movement of the water reflecting sunlight and blue sky is omnipresent and eternal.

This constant flow of water is like the steadfast flow of the love of God in our lives if we but step into the stream, sit, contemplate, and immerse ourselves in the flow. The river of God's steadfast love is always there waiting for our need, participation, and praise.

Playing with the current above the tiny waterfall, I held my palm up against the flow of water. The effect was to change the flow and the sound of the water as it sped over the rocks. This was a lesson too. Through immaturity, neglect, or sin, we can disrupt the flow of the steadfast love of God in our lives. When we do, it changes the direction of the flow and the sound that love makes in our hearts. It is possible to stand against the love of God, resisting its effects on our faith and life.

"There is a river whose streams make glad the city of God," the psalmist says. There is an ever-flowing river of God's steadfast love available to each of us.

We just have to get our feet wet.

Guided Prayer

Dear God,

I need your steadfast love in my life this day. I particularly need to know your love because _____

_____

_____.

In the past I have felt separated from your love, O God. What are the barriers that I have built?

I have come to depend on many things and people for a sense of goodness in my life. That your love is sufficient for me is a strange idea.

Lead me to immerse myself in your love that I may live out of it in Christian service to others. Amen.

CHRIST OUR LORD

Psalm 16

Daily Scripture

* Sunday:

A	B	C
Ezekiel 34:11-16, 20-24	2 Samuel 23:1-7	Jeremiah 23:1-6
Psalm 100	Psalm 132:1-12	Psalm 46
Ephesians 1:15-23	Revelation 1:4b-8	Colossians 1:11-20
Matthew 25:31-46	John 18:33-37	Luke 1:68-79, 23:33-43

* Monday:	John 11:17-27
* Tuesday:	Romans 10:1-13
* Wednesday:	2 Corinthians 5:14-21
* Thursday:	Ephesians 1:3-14
* Friday:	Philippians 2:1-13
* Saturday:	2 Timothy 2:8-26

Meditation

Church language surrounding the lordship of Christ sounds like we all know, understand, and agree about its meaning. But that may be a mistake. "Jesus Christ is Lord" is the common pledge at baptism for Protestants. And perhaps the most common phrase attached to the idea is "living under the lordship of Christ" or "finding the will of Christ for our lives."

Sometimes as Christians we flounder in our Christian discipleship because we don't really know what the phrase means or how we are to live out our lives. Sometimes, if we pay very careful attention to the Gospels, we realize the task of living with Jesus Christ as Lord is truly daunting and we settle for what is comfortable, for what doesn't seriously threaten our personal status quo.

To have Jesus Christ as Lord of our lives is to live with the Jesus of the Gospels made manifest in our daily lives. To live with Jesus

Christ as Lord is to be about the calling that Jesus defined by quoting Isaiah: "Bring good news to the poor...proclaim release to the captives and recovery of sight to the blind, to let the oppressed go free, to proclaim the year of the Lord's favor" (Luke 4:18-19).

To seek the lordship of Christ in our lives is to begin the day in prayer for God's direction for each day that we are given. The etymology of the word *lord* in English has a hint for us. It comes from a military term that referred to the office of steward who was in charge of the soldiers' provisions. So for us to acknowledge Jesus as lord of our lives is to acknowledge that God in Christ is the steward of what we need. It is to acknowledge that the spiritual provisions of our lives are what God in Christ wants to offer us. It is also to acknowledge that we are dependent on those provisions.

This is the rub for most American Christians. Our culture's historical emphasis on self-sufficiency and the contemporary emphasis on "getting our needs met" tends to tempt us away from the posture of dependency on spiritual provisions from God.

And our model, Jesus, spent so much time with unsavory people. That calling means that we spend most of our time with the poor, prisoners, those who are blind in some way, and those who are victims. That does not appeal to American Christians who feel the daily cultural pull toward personal success.

Discernment of the lordship of Jesus Christ in our lives is an individual matter. We have to sincerely seek God's leading; God is not going to force us into submission. Perhaps part of our prayer needs to be for the desire to seek the lordship of Jesus Christ in our lives.

Guided Prayer

Dear God,

I have used the words, "Jesus is Lord," all my life, God. You look on the heart and know when I have been sincere and when I have not.

I would renew my pledge. Show me the poor, the prisoners, the blind, and the victims who are waiting on my discipleship. I fear

my inability to _____

_____

_____.

Take away my attachment to success and comfort, that I may learn again that your yoke is easy when I seek the provisions you offer my life. In Jesus' name, Amen.